when you can't say

"Tell me, how are we two going to face the Day of Judgment? The sun is witness that it has gone down on our anger not one day, but for many a long year."

—From a letter written by St. Jerome
(who translated the Bible into Latin),
written to finally forgive and to seek forgiveness
from his aunt, from whom he'd been bitterly estranged

when you can't say "I

FORGIVE YOU"

Breaking the Bonds of
Anger and Hurt

GRACE KETTERMAN, M.D.
AND DAVID HAZARD

NAVPRESS

BRINGING TRUTH TO LIFE

P.O. Box 35001, Colorado Springs, Colorado 80935

OUR GUARANTEE TO YOU

We believe so strongly in the message of our books that we are making this quality guarantee to you. If for any reason you are disappointed with the content of this book, return the title page to us with your name and address and we will refund to you the list price of the book. To help us serve you better, please briefly describe why you were disappointed. Mail your refund request to: NavPress, P.O. Box 35002, Colorado Springs, CO 80935.

The Navigators is an international Christian organization. Our mission is to reach, disciple, and equip people to know Christ and to make Him known through successive generations. We envision multitudes of diverse people in the United States and every other nation who have a passionate love for Christ, live a lifestyle of sharing Christ's love, and multiply spiritual laborers among those without Christ.

NavPress is the publishing ministry of The Navigators. NavPress publications help believers learn biblical truth and apply what they learn to their lives and ministries. Our mission is to stimulate spiritual formation among our readers.

Library of Congress Catalog Card Number: 00-027185

ISBN 1-57683-037-3

Cover design by David Carlson Design
Cover photo by Joe Pellegrini

Creative Team: Jacqueline Blakely, Terry Behimer, and Vickie Howard

Some of the anecdotal illustrations in this book are true to life and are included with the permission of the persons involved. All other illustrations are composites of real situations, and any resemblance to people living or dead is coincidental.

Unless otherwise identified, all Scripture quotations in this publication are taken from the HOLY BIBLE: NEW INTERNATIONAL VERSION® (NIV®). Copyright © 1973, 1978, 1984 by International Bible Society. Used by permission of Zondervan Publishing House. All rights reserved. Other versions used include: *The New Testament in Modern English* (PH), J. B. Phillips Translator, © J. B. Phillips 1958, 1960, 1972, used by permission of Macmillan Publishing Company; and the *King James Version* (KJV).

Library of Congress Cataloging-in-Publication Data

Ketterman, Grace H.
      When you can't say "I forgive you" : breaking the bonds of anger and hurt / Grace H. Ketterman and David Hazard.
      p.cm.
      ISBN 1-57683-037-3 (pbk.)
      1. Forgiveness—Religious aspects—Christianity. I. Hazard, David. II. Title.

BV4647.F55 K48 2000
234'.5-dc21   00—027185

Printed in the United States of America

2 3 4 5 6 7 8 9 10 / 05 04 03 02 01

FOR A FREE CATALOG OF
NAVPRESS BOOKS & BIBLE STUDIES,
CALL 1-800-366-7788 (USA)
OR 1-416-499-4615 (CANADA)

To my husband, Herb, who taught me so much about forgiving,
and to our children, Kathy, Lyndon, and Wendy,
who taught us both even more!

and

To MaryLynne Hazard

CONTENTS

Introduction: Once There Was a Man . . .   11

CHAPTER

 One: When Forgiveness Is Impossible   15

 Two: What Cost Are You Willing to Pay?   27

 Three: Forgive, and You Will Be Forgiven   47

 Four: What Forgiveness Is Not   65

 Five: A Personal Reckoning   81

 Six: Strength for the Long Haul   103

 Seven: Eternity in View   121

 Eight: Forgiving Yourself   141

 Nine: Forgiving God   155

 Ten: Restoration   171

Notes   187

About the Authors   189

ONCE THERE WAS A MAN...

ONCE THERE WAS A MAN WHO STOOD UP ON A HILLSIDE and looked out over a crowd gathered to hear him speak. Gray were their faces, for they lived in a harsh, unforgiving land. He had something to give them—a map that would help them find their way to a whole new world . . . and a new life.

This man saw not only the drained-looking faces, but their very hearts—the memories that stored themselves in dark pockets and the very pulse that beat in blood and muscle. He saw . . .

- the sorrow of a woman who had been misused by men all her life, with no one to stand up for her
- the anger of a man who had been cheated by his employer, then let go
- the daily frustration and the crushed dreams of a young man crippled by someone's callous carelessness
- the unending anguish of an older woman still grieving for the child whose life was taken by someone who had escaped punishment

- the terror and rage of a small child left to fend for himself against bullying older brothers
- the shame of a teenaged boy—and near him a teenaged girl—sexually betrayed by someone dear and trusted

And seeing within them every hurt, sad, angry impulse, the man spoke in a loud voice, saying something like this: "The peace and happiness that come from God and lift the spirit can be yours, *if* you learn to free your soul from all that keeps you bound to this world—all the terrible things that happen to you here."*

It's likely many of his hearers were momentarily distracted, thinking, *How on earth can I find peace in this life? And happiness? Impossible. He has no idea how much I've been wronged, how much I've suffered and lost.* They couldn't see their own thoughts for what they were—invisible chains that imprisoned them.

But the man could also see in these hearts another impulse. More than anything, they wanted to know in their hearts that God was real . . . that he cared about their difficulties and could heal their wounds, setting their spirits free to live again. If this God was real, they wanted to know how to find their way to him.

Knowing this, the man told them the directions from his map, directions that didn't lead to a place but to the heart of God:

"Forgive, and then you'll know the peace and happiness that come from God. This is because forgiving someone a great debt allows you to understand both the heart of God *and* what he will pay so that you may be completely forgiven."

That day, some went down from the hillside unhappy. They were thinking, *Doesn't he know I've tried to forgive?* and *What good does forgiveness do?* and *I'd rather see my offender punished than live in heaven with a God who asks me to do the impossible.*

---

* We hope our readers can accept this Scripture rendering, and this story. They are offered in the fine tradition of Scripture interpretation that both reveres eternal truth and presents it in fresh and light-giving new ways.

But some followed the man from that day on. They said to him, "We *want* to know the peace that comes from God. But we don't know how to forgive, really. One day we try . . . and the next day we think of what was done to us, and all the old hurt, sadness, and anger come rushing back. Will you teach us how to really forgive . . . *from the heart?*"

And Jesus said, "Yes, I will."

Forgive . . . *from the heart.* That's the direction Jesus gave us. Forgiving and being forgiven are the way to a life with God's peace inside us — the peace of heaven that can replace the turmoil of the deep hurt, loss, betrayal, and anger driven into us in this world.

Yet in our many years of counseling people (Grace as a psychiatrist, David as a leader in both church and parachurch ministries), we've met so many who struggle to forgive. And certainly neither of us has been sheltered from this struggle. Forgiveness seems to be one of the greatest human challenges. And it's not made any easier, especially for believers, by those who wag a spiritual finger and say, "Just forgive. That's what God tells us to do." Well-meaning as these people may be, most do not seem to really grasp the depths of Jesus' teachings on forgiveness or understand that he pointed the way to a deep-heart process that is as freeing as it is challenging.

If you are like many people we know, you may want to be free of past offenses, but you still carry bitter memories of, or hard feelings toward, those who have wronged you. No one seems immune from this urge to carry offenses long after they've been committed, not the newest saint or the oldest. If you see their faces in your mind's eye right now, the voice of honesty within you says, *I can't say "I forgive you" because that would not be truthful. God tells me to. I believe I should. Maybe it would even be better for me if I did. But I know I haven't forgiven you for what you did to me. Right now I'm not sure I know whether I can, or how.*

From our own lives, and the lives of many we know, we want to assure you of this:

Forgiving even the worst offenses committed against you is not impossible.

Moreover, you can find freedom from the past, and peace that comes from God, by learning how to really forgive from the heart.

It's with that firm conviction that we ask you to join us on a journey into Jesus' teachings and into your own soul. We believe that as you take a look at his words presented in a fresh way, you will begin to discover freedom and healing from offenses of the past . . . and new maturity as a disciple of Jesus Christ.

CHAPTER ONE

WHEN FORGIVENESS IS IMPOSSIBLE

TOM DISCOVERED THAT LISA HAD BEEN UNFAITHFUL TO him, starting about seven months after they were married. Lisa wept and begged his forgiveness; she acknowledged she'd been stupid to fall for the come-ons of an old flame. After his rage cooled, his family, friends, and pastor all counseled Tom to give her another chance: "She's sorry. You need to forgive her, go through counseling together, and start over."

How do I forgive something that big? Tom wondered. *If I forgive, can I forget?* With his family and the church telling him to let go of his bitterness and move on, he told himself, *They have no idea how big this is. They're asking me to do the impossible.*

Susanne's struggle with hurt and anger was chronic. She saw her parents maybe three times a year, with a few phone chats in-between, and it was always the same: her father's cold indifference, broken only by his intolerance and criticisms; her mother's sweet but airy chatter, and her refusal to deal with Susanne's father as a responsible adult. *I hate this,* Susanne told herself. *How did I wind up with the most self-centered parents on earth? Why can't my kids have sane, caring grandparents?*

Susanne's husband kept telling her, "Just accept them the way they are." Her Christian friends asked, "Have you forgiven them?" Susanne found these words irritating. *Every time I try to forgive, they do the same things all over again—and I'm left with the same old pain, with some new pain to boot. The only way I could forgive them would be to stop seeing them, and that's not right either.*

Tom and Susanne face the same problem, though his situation is acute and hers is chronic. How can we forgive when great injury is done to us? Is it really possible to resolve the pain, grief, and anger? Can relationships badly damaged really be repaired?

And what if the offender isn't even around anymore? Carmen carried incredible sadness and anger for the father who chose his career as a navy commander, spending six months at a time out at sea and missing nearly every important event of Carmen's growing-up years. Now Carmen's dad is dead. Is there any way to resolve offenses in cases like that? Or consider Barbara, whose neighbor, gabbing on the phone while baby-sitting, allowed Barbara's two-year-old to drown in the bathtub. How can she forgive, surrounded by daily reminders that stir fresh pain for her lost child?

A Challenge . . . and a Chance

Massive hurt. Bitter disappointment. Betrayal. Unspeakable sadness. Painful rejection at another's indifference to us. In the "range" of human emotions, these are the Himalayas. We look at others with their garden-variety complaints about life and wish we had their problems rather than ours. We could easily forgive little insults, forgotten invitations or anniversaries, a bit of gossip; it's not that we're "forgiveness impaired." But just as we don't meet seasoned, expert mountaineers who've climbed Mount Everest every day, we don't often meet people who've been challenged to scale the high peaks of offense that seem to block our way in life.

You already have the challenge: *How can one forgive when for-*

giveness seems impossible? Trying to ignore and walk away from feelings of unforgiveness just doesn't work. They're always there, like a soaring mountain range, seemingly impassable—therefore, they hold us back spiritually and emotionally. Saying it's not fair that these circumstances happened to us is moot. There they are. What we're offering is a chance—a chance to find a way over and beyond circumstances that seem impossible to forgive.

On the other side is the restored peace, stability, and spiritual maturity that may also seem impossible to reach right now. And something more.

If we count ourselves as active followers of Jesus Christ, we can carry an added weight on top of the offenses we cannot seem to resolve or let go. We know very well that Jesus told us, "Forgive, and you will be forgiven" (Luke 6:37). But if we've been unable to do this, we can carry guilt that we haven't obeyed Christ in this most basic instruction. The fact that others keep prompting us to forgive only adds to the pressure, amplifying our shortcoming.

We want to walk you through steps that will not only set you free from painful emotions, but teach you the *process* of forgiveness. You should know right now that others who are pressing you to "just forgive" quite likely do not understand this process—or even that forgiveness *is* a process—because they haven't been challenged by circumstances that are this enormous and emotionally "impassable." (As the *Washington Post* newspaper says in its advertising, "If you don't get it, you just don't get it.")

In our years of working with people struggling to forgive, we've encountered many who felt trapped in unforgiveness. From their tough and amazing experiences, and from our own, we can tell you it is possible to forgive when it seems impossible. Not only that, but forgiving is a chance to personally experience God's miraculous, transforming grace more profoundly than you ever thought possible.

Do you want to be free within? Do you want to know and

experience God more intimately? Then commit yourself now to this journey with us through the process of forgiveness.

To offer you a glimpse of the road ahead, we want to tell you about Lori and Kevin, who came to Grace for help when their situation was at its bleakest.

I Can't . . . I Won't!

Grace noticed that Lori's dark brown eyes, usually sparkling, were dull. Lori avoided Grace's gaze, signaling that something big was up. Kevin, Lori's husband, sat silent and tense in a chair across the room, with fire in his eyes. Grace knew her question had hit a nerve.

"How are things between you and Kevin?" she repeated, and waited in the long silence for a reply. They'd come insisting they had "a solid commitment to marriage." But both had dealt the other massive hurts and bitter disappointments. In this case, neither one believed it was possible to forgive. As their counselor, Grace knew that forgiveness was *exactly* what they needed if they were to be released from the past and go on to experience spiritual, emotional, and even physical health. Without going through the process of forgiveness, they'd fail to thrive in healthy ways, and wrongs done to them in the past would infect their future.

Suddenly, Lori looked up. "The truth is, I can't stand the sight of Kevin anymore," she confessed. Then came a catalog of all the hassles and hurts of some twelve years together. She *hated* Kevin's immaturity, his temper, his self-centeredness . . . (Having heard both sides many times, Grace knew there were two sides to the story, but allowed Lori to vent.) Then she dropped the bomb: "I want *out* of this marriage."

"Do you really mean that, Lori," Grace asked, "or do you mean you want out of the *kind* of marriage you've had? That you want to move on to a new phase of *this* marriage? Because that's possible if . . . "

"No," she interrupted. "I mean *out*," she insisted. "In fact, I've already moved out. And I'm *not* going back."

Kevin had listened as long as he could stand it. His face coloring, he jumped in. "She can't *do* this to me and the boys. She can't just give up and walk out on us." Angrily, he described the emotional roller coaster he'd been on since she'd cut him off, a plunge from rage to deep grief to numbing depression.

"And what about our marriage vows—'till death do us part'?" he shot at Lori. Turning to Grace, he pleaded, "Tell her what she did is wrong. She ripped our family apart. The pain on the boys' faces is unbearable. And when I think about the possibility of her meeting another man ... I ... " The words and pent-up fury caught in his throat.

When Grace asked Kevin how he was handling all these intense emotions, his fists clenched. He admitted considering suicide ... murder ... or both ... then waved these aside. "It's just the anger talking. I'd never do anything like that. But she has to come back."

Venturing into new, risky territory, Grace asked, "Lori, can you *forgive* Kevin for the things you see wrong with him? And Kevin, can you forgive Lori for her shortcomings, and for the pain she's caused by moving out?"

Both heads snapped. "*Forgive?*" Lori's bottom-line was instantaneous, while Kevin rehashed his long list of bitter complaints—and both wound up at much the same place. "I can't ... I won't!"

These two are like most of us when it comes to dealing with life's hard challenges. We confuse "*I can't*"—our sense that a challenge is too hard and lies beyond our ability—with "*I won't*"—our refusal to *work*, or a feeling that it's too much or too unfair to be asked to stretch, reach, and grow in order to meet that challenge. As long as Lori and Kevin remained in this immature mindset, their situation was grave indeed—and seemingly hopeless.

RESISTANCE

Grace's new suggestion met with a lot of emotional energy, as Kevin and Lori traded excuses and explanations of why forgiving was impossible: "Am I supposed to pretend I don't absolutely *hate* it when Kevin gets angry and acts like a child?" "She has belittled me for years, yet never sees her own immaturity. And now she's traumatized our boys by walking out on them. Do I just pretend all that didn't happen?"

"Actually," Grace clarified, "I want to rephrase my question. I asked, '*Can* you forgive?'—but I wasn't asking about your emotional state, as in, 'Do you *feel* in a forgiving mood?' or 'Are you willing *right now?*' I want to know whether you're willing to make a mature, adult choice, whether you feel like it or not. I want to ask, 'Are you *willing to become willing* to forgive?'"

Significantly, neither one asked the next logical question: "How can I become willing? How can I work at redirecting my will?"

When we choose to take any strong position—whether an external position, like a job, or an internal position, like unforgiveness—we throw enormous interior energy into *defending* and *holding* that position. We tell ourselves it's right and "for the best," or it's all we know to do. In short, we work hard to justify our choice. What happens if someone suggests a new position? We immediately sense what it's going to cost us in terms of inner energy—that is, a lot of work! It will cost us interior unease as we move away from a choice that felt stable toward a new position that's unsure (because we haven't moved into it yet). It will cost us mental and emotional energy. We sense there will be bigger costs, too. It's important to make this point:

When any of us is faced with a new thought, especially a concept that challenges us to move from one level of maturity to another, we put up a lot of inner resistance. The energy, time, and verbiage we expend in this resistance can be tremendous. The immature part of us wants only what it *feels* like it wants, and it doesn't want to work to achieve something new. *Period.*

In Kevin and Lori's case, both were battling hard to hold onto their positions as the aggrieved party, and neither seemed interested in achieving anything new. As the session ended in a charged atmosphere of hurt, distrust, and rage, Grace could only pray that something would break through their inner walls of resistance and allow them to catch a glimpse of new possibilities . . . of the more spiritually mature and whole people they could become.

FARTHER THAN WE'VE GONE BEFORE

The difficulty any of us has in breaking through to a new way of living is that it does require us to undergo stretching and discomfort. This inner work is what we avoid at all costs. But every time we do the work of stretching and facing our discomfort, we become wiser, more mature, than we were before. Learning to forgive when it seems impossible is nothing less than a strenuous workout for the inner being. It is the inner work that frees us from the past *and* makes us stronger, wiser, more whole individuals.

Most of us would say we want to grow, mature, and become whole adults. As Christians we say we want to be more godly, more like Jesus Christ, obeying God by learning to forgive. But why is spiritual growth so hard?

It can be helpful to look at what it takes to learn a mechanical skill like plumbing or playing the piano. You may try to install a sink for the first time and wind up with water running over the floor—*or* with a new fixture where you need it, plus a healthy sense of accomplishment to boot. You may agree to practice for your first public recital and wind up in front of a crowd with your fingers frozen over the keyboard—*or* with a confidence that comes from mastering your fear and creating music good enough to be enjoyed. The *or* part is the problem. The risk is that we won't wind up with what we want, and the "insecurity alarm" goes off. When it comes to forgiveness, what if we take the risk and offer it, and it doesn't *do* what we want it to do? What if it doesn't resolve the issue? What if it only allows the offender to get close again, only to pull the same thing and injure us once more? (We'll consider these issues in later chapters.)

Here's the catch in stepping into new territory: In order to grow, we have to put aside the natural resistance that comes when we feel insecure and uncomfortable. Feeling uncomfortable and unsteady is *normal* when we're being challenged to step out of our old comfort zone and risk. The question is, Will we perpetually allow ourselves to shy away from the discomfort? Or will we accept that growth always involves urging ourselves to go farther than we've had to go before?

A sense of unsteadiness and uncertainty is the inner ground that growth requires us to cross. *It's also the point where our struggle begins in dead earnest.*

Because we resist what is uncomfortable, all growth tends to begin with a huge struggle. On one side of the struggle is our present way of seeing and doing things and even our basic personhood—which form our sense of what is *fair, just,* and *right.* To change this sense of *rightness* is to change our spiritual equilibrium, and it is accomplished only by a fight to the death. Why? Because to change in a deep way means more than simply *learning something new*—it requires us to *become someone new.* The person we are within, with our old way of seeing, thinking, and acting, must "die" in order to let a "new" person be spiritually born within.

This all makes sense on paper, doesn't it? But our challenge to grow spiritually isn't at its peak when we're sitting in an armchair reading a book, even the Bible. *Spiritual growth only happens in the trenches of real life.* And moreover, *our greatest challenges, and our greatest need to change and grow, usually come in the areas where we least want to be challenged.*

What happened next for Lori and Kevin illustrates what we mean.

SURPRISED BY THE IMPOSSIBLE

Starting over with Kevin was not on Lori's agenda. Shortly after moving out, she filed for divorce. Then, odd as it may seem, Grace's prayer for a breakthrough was answered when a near-tragedy occurred.

One night, in a fit of anger and despair, Kevin did something violent that might have cost him his life. The next time these two saw each other, Kevin lay swathed in bandages. For his part, Kevin was still despairing, but was also shaken by the incident; his sons could have been fatherless. As for Lori, something about Kevin's physical suffering got through to her in a way that nothing else could. The sad look on his face said he loved her so much he'd all but given up on life rather than face a future without her.

Still, the old, angry, entrenched side of Lori tried to fight off these feelings. Wasn't it just like Kevin to let his emotions get out of hand and do something stupid to injure himself?

But the angry, negative feelings were losing their power. *Maybe,* she thought grudgingly, *I was wrong to be so unforgiving. . . .*

What was it in Lori that changed?

For just a moment, she had been jolted by the reality of Kevin's pain. She climbed out of her self-protective foxhole in this emotional war and saw life from Kevin's point of view. With the energy of her own negative emotions temporarily shut down, she caught a new glimpse of Kevin, spiritually speaking, by feeling a little of what he was feeling. By getting outside of herself, by experiencing feelings other than her own, Lori had stretched and grown just a little.

In her case, we believe, Providence had allowed her to glimpse and experience just enough.

When Lori left Kevin that day, something long dead flickered back to life. Not a feeling, exactly. A *conviction.* Kevin was not a two-dimensional cutout of an "angry, immature guy." That's what she had reduced him to in her mind. He had a loving, deeply caring side that she'd fallen in love with years before. She'd lost sight of that. She'd buried Kevin's good side beneath a stack of charges against him as, year after year, she kept tallying up all the things he did that were wrong in her eyes. Not that she was completely wrong in her assessment of Kevin's immaturity—but an unguarded moment of empathy had shown her she wasn't all *right* either.

At the same time, Kevin was experiencing his own changes. He was jolted into reality by what he'd done to himself. That shock caused him to step out of his own skin long enough to see himself from another viewpoint. Isn't all uncontrolled anger the act of a hurt, frustrated child who can't get his way? He felt so foolish. Lori wasn't responsible for *this* tragic mess—he was. Maybe he needed to be responsible and grow up, just as Lori had been saying forever.

In his own way, Kevin also experienced what it was like to step into someone else's shoes and feel what that person felt. From that moment of revelation, things began to change for this couple. The situation began to change because the two people in it were changed.

A New Heart, a New Start

In time, with efforts to rebuild, healing came. Lori called off divorce proceedings, and they began to restore their family unity. In truth, their story could have ended much differently. What if only one party had experienced a deep change of heart? In our imperfect world, wonderful reconciliations don't occur as often as we'd all like.

But a true miracle occurs in the life of the one who learns to forgive—something so profoundly healing that it does not matter, in one sense, whether reconciliation takes place or not. The healing of the relationship is one of the goals we can stay open to as Christians. But personal spiritual freedom does not depend on it. Any one of us can move on and grow toward inner maturity and wholeness, *even if the one who harmed us never does.*

It's important to understand that we're not going to arm you with persuasive techniques that will get the offender to admit he was wrong and repay the debt he owes you.

We know from counseling others—and from our own experiences—the strength and freedom that can be ours by learning how to forgive. There are important steps in the process of forgiving major offenses, as you may have picked up in Lori and Kevin's story. Choosing to follow them sets you on a path toward wholeness. In this way you are "free indeed," just as Jesus promised (John 8:36), and not left at the mercy of what the offender does or doesn't do.

Perhaps someone has crippled your spirit with years of withering criticism, unfairness, blame, and rejection. Maybe the most important people in your life have betrayed you by their lies, neglect, abuse, or abandonment. Perhaps you have suffered an excruciating loss—of a marriage, a career, even the life of a child or spouse—at someone's hands. Adding insult to injury, the offender may never show one bit of remorse.

The harm and wounding that we all suffer in this life seem endless. Jesus knew that when He taught about the critical importance of forgiveness. He was not naive—He knew very well what it costs us to forgive and let go of the injuries done to us. At the same time, He knew what it costs us *not* to forgive. Because Jesus was the master of forgiveness and because His teachings on forgiveness are sometimes misunderstood, we'll look at them as we begin the next chapter.

FORGIVENESS IS ESSENTIAL

Because there is no end of grief that comes *to* us, forgiveness is not just a "good idea" or "a nice Christian thing to do." It's an essential of life. If we follow the path of forgiveness that Jesus taught, there can be a definite end to the harm that comes *from* the painful events of our past. We can stop the past from robbing our future.

You can be healed and set free as you learn to walk the wonderful path of forgiveness. The gifts of personal wholeness in Jesus Christ can be yours, even when you think forgiveness is impossible.

The only question now is — *are you willing to begin?*

CHAPTER TWO

WHAT COST ARE YOU WILLING TO PAY?

PERHAPS YOU'VE NOTICED THAT FORGIVENESS IS OFTEN IN THE news these days, as psychologists and even political figures are rediscovering the power of this ancient way to resolve conflicts. Bishop Desmond Tutu, the black Anglican leader in South Africa, has shown that forgiveness can help to heal the soul of a whole nation, even when the most horrific atrocities have occurred.

Bishop Tutu has said, "Forgiveness is always in my best interest, though it does not seem so at first. [Forgiveness] brings us both to wholeness."[1]

He also has stated that forgiveness has kept South Africa from a bloodbath of retribution after the ending of white domination. Yet most of us shake our heads and reject that notion without making any effort to understand how such a social and political miracle could take place.

Why is it so hard to understand the way of forgiveness? Why do we look at those who forgive as weak or foolish, or as "natural born saints" who can do spiritually impossible things we mere mortals just can't do? Why does forgiveness seem so impossible to us?

FORGIVENESS JUST ISN'T NATURAL

Jesus Christ is the master of forgiveness.

Yet it seems that the power and profound depths of His teaching on forgiveness are not understood, and are actually mis-understood—even by faithful people.

Jesus' insights into the soul are central to this book because they lead to inner health and spiritual freedom like nothing else we know.

It seems that human beings have always had trouble with the idea of forgiving someone who has wronged them. It's just not natural to us.

But Jesus came to show us that there is a *supernatural* way to live. Sometimes we get hung up on that word—supernatural—and think it refers only to mystical happenings and those sudden miracles in which physical reality is altered in an instant of time. Actually, it has a meaning that's much more accessible. On a practical human level, Jesus came to teach us how to adopt *new attitudes of the heart* that help us to live "above" our natural impulses. Because these heart attitudes help us to develop a new nature—what theologians would call *godly character* or *the character of Christ*—they condition us to react in ways that *supercede* our old, natural ways of responding to life.

Learning to govern our old nature is, we believe, what Jesus' apostles meant when they told us about the kind of spiritual living that "overcomes the world" and transforms the inner being (see 2 Peter 1:4; 1 John 5:4). We also believe this requires something more than simple psychological mechanics or a spiritualized way of referring to behavior therapy. Rather, when we learn how to make these godly attitudes ours, we actually experience God's Spirit and His life in us at a profound level of our being. As the apostle Peter taught, we actually "participate in the divine nature" (2 Peter 1:4).

It appears that Jesus came to teach us about a way to live so that the living Spirit of God can touch us deep within and transfuse us with new life, giving us strengths and capabilities we didn't have before. In this way, we can be changed from the inside out and allow a new higher nature to be born in us and eventually replace our first nature. (We'll consider the "eventually" part as we look at the process of spiritual growth and maturity later.)

WELL AND GOOD, BUT . . .

All of this sounds fine, doesn't it? The problem is, the change that needs to occur in us must take place at the deepest level of our being.

In the first chapter, we began to consider why forgiveness seems so impossible, so unnatural and even godlike to us. To understand why this is so, it's important to look deep into the human soul.

Few reactions are more elemental to human nature than the impulse to take revenge, to punish someone who has done us harm. This reaction is automatic, instantaneous, and reflexive in human nature. It's known as the *talionic impulse.* The term comes from a root word that means "to punish in a way that exacts a penalty corresponding in kind to the crime . . . as in the principle of an eye for an eye."[2] From this root we also get the word *retaliate,* which refers to our innate impulse to strike back, to make someone else repay with an "eye for an eye, a tooth for a tooth"—and, frankly, even more if we can get it.

Forgive? The impulse to retaliate is so deeply ingrained in the world's attitude that many of us have accepted the idea that we're weak if we come out of a fight and can't say, "I gave as good as I got." This impulse has far greater impact on our lives than we think. Its strength and energy are so virulent that they affect us all—even those of us who consider ourselves "good" and "mild-mannered" people, and those of us who can override our impulses because we're smart enough to recognize situations in which it's not wise to retaliate.

Let's say your boss puts you down in a morning staff meeting. If you were attacked with a knife, you wouldn't hesitate to fight for your life—but you've been trained (hopefully) since you were small to override your first impulse to strike out at *every attack*. Remember learning that "sticks and stones may break your bones, but names can never hurt you"? We're trained by parents and teachers to keep quiet and not dish out a put-down or challenge in response to an attack. We are taught that retaliation may in fact be the worst thing to do in social conflicts, in which one's life is not actually at stake.

And so a *second* impulse checks the first instinct. It's still a self-preservation response, but this one is refined by social training and reminds you that an overt confrontation would endanger your chance for advancement or a raise, or maybe cost you your job. So instead of retaliating, you give a reasonable response—or at least keep your mouth shut and don't confront the boss in a room full of coworkers!

We want you to notice two things from this simple illustration. First, every one of us can recognize that it's sometimes in our best interest not to retaliate on impulse. Second, it's not as impossible as we insist to both override and retrain the natural impulse to retaliate!

ALL THAT ENERGY

However, even if we temporarily divert the retaliation impulse, it will continue to energize us in some way. Merely "containing" or "stuffing" hurt and anger is not the same as *dealing with it* in healthy and mature ways. When we contain, it's only a matter of time and opportunity before most of us will find a "safer" way to vent those pent-up energies we feel toward the person who offended us. All that energy has to have someplace to go.

Let's go back to the illustration we used earlier about your boss berating you in a morning meeting. Over lunch, away from the office, perhaps you verbally beat up on the boss in his absence by means of gossip and slander. Maybe you even color the truth to make him look *really* bad. Perhaps you also find ways to undermine the boss's efforts, or even covertly harm them, by dragging your feet on a project or withholding vital information. Maybe, thinking you're doing the right thing, you contain your anger for good, sealing it inside, by judging yourself to be superior and the boss to be worthless.

Don't be fooled: If hurt and anger are not replaced with another kind of spiritual and emotional energy, the impulse to retaliate *will* find a way to work outward from our spirit, or to stay locked up inside us, where it poisons our inner atmosphere. In the end, it will deliver some kind of a slap to the face! In the drive to get "an eye for an eye," we *will* wound and penalize the other person somehow.

But the drive to get even only equalizes the score temporarily; it does not *settle* the score. Even "justifiable" retaliation only brings defensiveness and new strikes against us. Why? Because we all have a tendency to feel justified in what we say and do, even if it hurts someone else, and to feel unfairly misunderstood and mistreated when others hurt us.

At the bottom of it all, *no one ever feels the score really is even!* Relational war games go on without end, usually escalating until there is a "winner" and a "loser," or until the parties separate to protect themselves from mutual destruction. This need for a definite winner and a loser—the need to see ourselves and our position as *right*—is one of the greatest of those "Himalayan peaks" that hold us back.

THE COST OF BITTER CONFLICT

Jesus came to free us and show us a new way to get beyond the endless and escalating nature of the retaliation impulse. Only if you first understand its malignant nature will you understand how urgent and powerful is His teaching on forgiveness. We're mistaken if we think Jesus' teaching was namby-pamby, some weak attempt to make the world "sweeter." He came to shed light on the terrible force we turn loose in the world when we retaliate, and the cost we pay *personally* when we insist we cannot forgive.

The truth He came to teach us is this: The satisfaction that dishing out payback and punishment gives is only temporary. Far more real are the penalties and losses exacted in us when we will not learn the truth about forgiveness and how to forgive.

It's time to consider the great cost we're paying when we don't learn what Jesus came to teach about the miracle of forgiving.

Many health-care professionals are writing about the physiological costs of unresolved anger, bitterness, and lasting grief that remain toxic within us when we're unforgiving. We are, in a true sense, racked by the effects of unforgiveness, which cause our physical bodies to go through punishments almost as severe as what torture victims endure. The physical costs of unforgiveness may include hypertension, chronic headaches, high blood pressure, cardiovascular ailments, and gastrointestinal disorders, to name just a handful. Because negative emotions have a depressive effect and can suppress immune function, unforgiveness may even have an indirect link to major and severe disorders like rheumatoid arthritis and cancer.

Others have already written about these costs of unforgiveness. We don't repeat them here to be redundant or to scare you into forgiving (even if that could be done). We mention them only because we believe these physiological outworkings of unforgiveness give us visible proof of the truly virulent force at work within us when we don't move through and beyond offenses from the past. Jesus not only understood these costs, but taught how to move beyond them.

The dangerous force we want to expose is something that lies deeper in us than even the impulse to retaliate. It's what forms and unleashes that impulse, the way gathered storm clouds unleash lightning. We're referring to a mindset—an "inner climate," if you will. For our purposes here, we'll refer to it as the *legalistic mindset*.

We're aware that using the terms *legalistic* and *legalist* will present an obstacle.

First of all, when you see these terms you most likely immediately resist the notion that they could refer to you. Most of us tend to think that a *legalist* is someone who is always loudly demanding that others live and die by the rules—especially *his or her* rules. But we use these words to refer to those who think that exacting some kind of payback or punishment is the *only* way to deal with a person who's broken the rules as he or she sees them. When we're seriously wronged, the legalist latent in every one of us quickly rears its head. But the *persona* of the legalist is hard to see in ourselves; if we do see it, it's difficult to see why it isn't just the *right* way to be, why the world wouldn't be better off if more people were as exacting as we are!

A second problem with using these terms is the discourtesy we do to people when we reduce them to a label. Labeling has a way of keeping people stuck in a certain position, and we certainly do not mean to do that. On the contrary, though, *identifying,* in terms of starting with a baseline diagnosis, is helpful if we're looking for a treatment and desiring to move on to health. That, of course, is what we hope will happen.

What is the nature of legalism? Why is it so virulent? What happens within us when we fail to recognize it at work within us? What happens in our relationships with others? In our relationship with God?

Sadly, the legalistic mindset we're talking about is like a cancer that grows unseen within, doing incredible damage to us long before we recognize it.

Let's start by looking at some men that few of us would object to labeling as *legalists*—the Pharisees of Jesus' day. Maybe by looking into their exaggerated legalism, as in a distant mirror, we can spot certain native tendencies in our own thinking and behavior. Then we will consider the new and better way Jesus offered them.

THE INFECTION OF LEGALISM

In the New Testament we read that Jesus healed a paralyzed man while a whole crowd of everyday people and religious leaders looked on. As He was healing the man's body He said, "Friend, your sins are forgiven" (Luke 5:20).

We believe Jesus knew what He was doing when He both healed the man physically *and* told him his sins were forgiven. We know his paralysis surely kept him from working and serving his community and family well. Those of us who have known the paralyzing guilt that sin brings can imagine what shame kept him from doing. Jesus freed him in body and spirit, and now time would tell.

It's no surprise that the man, who'd been paralyzed for many years, was elated. And you can almost feel the uplifting force of wonder and hope that must have swept over the crowd. They were amazed at the healing because it was given *freely*. According to the laws found in Leviticus, those who experienced healing from physical ailments were to go and offer a sacrifice to God. The priests would judge whether it was an acceptable offering—whether it was the *right* offering, and *enough* of it—and, if so, pronounce forgiveness. *According to this mindset, you pay for forgiveness.*

Only if we understand this system and the mindset it produced will we understand why the religious leaders were instantly offended. *Who is this man,* they wondered, *to forgive anyone's sins?* (5:21). In their minds no one was released from the debt that came from even the smallest infraction—not until it was fully paid for and justice was satisfied.

Who were these men? What were they like? From a spiritual and psychological standpoint, they were men in whom the talionic impulse, that need to seek payback, was keenly honed and elevated to the status of a religion. For them, the law was no longer a God-given guide for right social and spiritual boundaries—the law had *become* God to them. Nowhere in the New Testament do you hear them referring to counterbalancing statements God had often made through Old Testament prophets about *mercy*.

As these teachers of the law saw it, their part was not only to keep the law themselves but to keep a sharp eye out for others who failed. They dealt severely with "offenders," leveling punishments and penalties, making sure they paid "enough" to compensate for their wrongdoing. Throughout the New Testament you find these same men harassing, driving away, and even stoning to death anyone who committed the slightest offense against their laws—even those who merely disagreed with them and "offended" their thinking. They could, and did, make life miserable for anyone who did not do right in their eyes.

In short, all their impulses came as quickly and deadly as lightning bolts from inner beings in which the law had been overemphasized to the exclusion of mercy, until their response to everything was exaggerated into an inner state, or spirit, of *legalism*. Unlike Jesus, there was no impulse in them to forgive freely.

It's interesting to notice how Jesus therapeutically confronted the unbalanced and legalistic spirit in these men. It's also important for us to understand the traits of this spirit so that we can see how we are affected when an offense gives it energy and causes it to grow out of balance.

ANATOMY OF A LEGALISTIC SPIRIT

As we've seen, the moment Jesus told the man in Luke 5 that his sins were forgiven, the religious leaders were offended. Because He knew the legalistic spirit so well, Jesus understood that they were experiencing great inner disturbance (5:22). So He asked a question that must have startled and confronted them: "Why are you thinking these things in your hearts? Which is easier: to say, 'Your sins are forgiven,' or to say, 'Get up and walk'?" (5:22-23).

They apparently did not know how to reply. The truth is, *neither* statement would have been easy for these men. They obviously did not have the power to heal someone miraculously, so to speak those words and see the man released from paralysis would have been impossible. On the other hand, it was well within their human power to say, "Your sins are forgiven and not held against you," and to be rewarded by witnessing the relief and gratitude those words bring. But they could not say those words.

The first trait of the legalistic spirit revealed in this confrontation is this: Unless the offender has paid some exacting penalty, it's *impossible* to say "I forgive you" and to release someone from the "debt" you believe they owe.

Frequently, Grace counsels couples in the aftermath of an affair. Let's say the husband is the offending party, and now he's remorseful and really wants to restore the marriage and even to make it better than before. Among other things, Grace asks the wife, "Because he's asking for your forgiveness, can you forgive him?" "Oh sure, I can forgive him," she's likely to respond. "But you can't expect me to forgive just like that. I'm going to make him *pay* first." Many are not that direct. But most exact payback from the spouse in some way—for instance, by forcing the spouse to give in on something he or she would never agree to otherwise.

We have purposely waited until this moment to introduce the definition of forgiveness. It's important to place its actual meaning in contrast to what most of us mean when we use the word. To forgive means: *To pardon; to absolve; to give up resentment of; to grant relief from payment of.*[3]

To the legalistic spirit, absolving someone of payment or penalty is way beyond the realm of possibility. It's too miraculous. How could anyone even ask us to do such an absurd thing? The teachers of the law insisted that only God can forgive sins—*even though they, of all people, should have known there is no place in their Scriptures where such a statement is made!* In many places, the so-called "angry, punishing" God of the Old Testament not only shows mercy, but encourages His people to offer mercy, too. But because forgiveness was so impossible to these men, they'd come to believe it was a right and a power that belonged only to God.

Someone trapped inside a legalistic spirit truly believes forgiveness is simply beyond human capability. To ask that person to forgive is to require a feat only "supersaints" can perform, or something patently absurd.

The second trait of the legalistic spirit that Jesus' confrontation brings to light is this: The legalistic spirit is focused on faultfinding, and grows more and more critical over time.

It is truly sad that these teachers of the law didn't speak one word of praise *or* objection to the physical healing Jesus performed. It was as though they didn't even notice the miracle, the wonder, the physiological impossibility that had just occurred before their eyes. They overlooked it totally because they were so focused on looking for something wrong.

Marc, an acquaintance of David's, complained about how stubborn, willful, sloppy, and lazy his daughter was. She was just entering puberty, a terribly difficult transitional time for most children—and a time when they most need parental support and acceptance. And yet, because so many "childish" traits are intermingled with adult-like demands, young people in this transition are very likely to do obnoxious things. And it's these obnoxious behaviors that can make them hard to take. Yet support and acceptance are what they need to get them through the transition.

With this in mind, David said to Marc, "Your daughter needs you to find something in her that deserves praise. If you praise her, you'll win her heart and it will be easier for her to take your suggestions and constructive criticism."

"You don't get it," he shot back. "There's nothing to praise."

There is no one in whom there is nothing to praise. Yet no suggestion that this father speak a kind, supportive word to his child *just because she was his own* could make a dent. Here was a man whose acceptance—and undoubtedly his forgiveness—was purely conditional. The people in his life would have to *earn* every word of praise, and the smallest measure of forgiveness. We guess that they receive precious little of either.

Here's the point: The legalistic spirit causes us to focus on the negative in others. We find it awkward, uncomfortable, or unnatural—if not impossible—to comment on positive traits. As this negative focus becomes a habit, the positive and the good in others slowly become invisible.

A TRAP OF OUR OWN MAKING

Before we consider the next trait of the legalistic spirit, we want to point out a problem the legalistic mindset causes for us—something we're usually blind to. Without counterbalancing influences, the mindset that demands that others live by and live up to our sense of right and wrong becomes stronger and leads to habitual negative thinking and actions. No matter how "nice" or "kind" we may appear on the outside, its virulence can be at work inside us. We zero in on someone who has offended us, and our words and actions are motivated by a harbored desire to bring harm.

The third trait of the legalistic spirit is that we not only see all the faults that exist in a person (and in all people in general), we may even see faults that are not there. In religious terms, we are becoming almost entirely *sin-focused*.

Elsewhere in the Gospels, the teachers of the law harass Jesus and His men for walking through a field of ripened grain and breaking off a few heads of grain to eat. They confront Jesus angrily, accusing Him and His men of "harvesting" on the Sabbath, which was "unlawful" (Luke 6:1-2). Since when is picking a few heads of grain "harvesting"? By habitually criticizing and faultfinding, these men had strengthened, or *amplified*, the legalistic spirit. Now it was actively, aggressively on the lookout for even hints of "sin" and wrongdoing.

Most of us will have a very hard time identifying this hyper-critical trait in ourselves. And yet it's there, or potentially there, in every one of us.

This trait is easiest to spot when we think of one person as our nemesis, or archrival. Jean viewed her older sister this way. She was extremely competitive with this sister, and for some reason felt she had to "better" her sister in terms of life accomplishments. The older sister was unaware of this drive in Jean, or at least she ignored it. Nonetheless, Jean seethed as she spoke about her older sibling: "She always calls and tells me how great her kids are doing in school, how excited she is about the research she's doing for her doctorate, and how quickly her husband is advancing in his career. She only tells me these things to rub my face in her success."

Whenever Jean's husband heard her speak like this, he stared in shock. "I can't even believe what I'm hearing. Your sister has never been anything but kind to us. She and [her husband] offer to let us use their condo at the beach every year and never ask for a penny."

"She only does that," Jean interrupted, "as a way of saying, 'We have something you don't have.'"

In this way, every conversation, every offer, was dissected with Jean's idea of right and wrong as she searched for evidence that her sister was nothing but a prideful braggart who maliciously paraded successes in a deliberate attempt to point out what a "failure" Jean was. When Jean was through, her sister's character was essentially butchered.

It's more common, perhaps, for us to be hypercritical and unforgiving of *one particular trait* that we don't like in a certain person, or in people in general.

Jerry admitted it "drove him up the wall" when his wife Carole felt hurt by him or by one of her friends. "It seems like *self-pity* to me — and I hate that." If Carole expressed even the mildest disappointment, she was treated with a self-righteous lecture, mocking, or a blast of anger. Years of Jerry's hypercritical responses to the smallest mentions of hurt by his wife or their children had almost totally destroyed their love for him.

Unfortunately, this destructive energy is widespread in

marriages. Many times we've listened to husbands and wives who've come for counseling or prayer, each one airing a host of complaints and criticisms about his or her spouse as if describing Joseph Stalin or Lizzie Borden! They blink when asked, "Is there anything *good* about your spouse? Does this person do *anything* right? Is there *any* reason at all to think well of him [her]?" "Sure," they say, "*but . . .* " Then off they go, rehashing the same long list of negatives as if we'd missed it the first time.

The person who has succumbed to the legalistic spirit and allowed the energy of hypercriticism to drive her believes that if she just bears down a little harder on the flaws of her spouse or children or friend, the "offender" will see and fix the flaws. Tragically, this chronic grinding only destroys relationships. In the end, it erodes one's relationship with God, as we'll see.

CRIMES AGAINST OUR BEING

Before we move on, we want to point out that hypercriticism can also take over when a truly serious or criminal offense has taken place—for instance, when someone has been abused emotionally or physically, or when serious betrayal and critical wounding have occurred. We believe it's important to look at this because the ability to move through and beyond crimes against our person and our being is hindered when we become stuck in the trap of legalism and devolve into a hypercritical state.

We don't mean that everyone who has experienced these things becomes hypercritical in the sense that they become outwardly nasty. But we do mean there is a tendency to be *hyperaware* of offenses—even possible offenses, and even conditions under which the same offense could occur again. We're not saying it's wrong to be cautious and even self-protective to a degree. But it's often the case that a person who has been so wounded can come to live, naturally so, inside an inner climate of fear and distrust. And it is this climate that works against the formation of healthy relationships *from that point into the future.*

For both the chronically and critically injured, it is nearly impossible to see that anything but punishing these and all offenders will help to transform the inward pain and calm the inner unease.[4]

A Hard Heart Is a Restless Heart

Whether we focus intensely and continuously on one individual or on certain traits we dislike, or on a terrible experience, we allow an unhealthy and destructive force to run loose in our lives and relationships.

This brings us to the fourth trait of the legalistic spirit: It encourages the development of a certain *hardness.* This can be mistaken for otherwise healthy traits like "conviction," "firmness," or "resolve"—or even "tough love." It can be applauded as a determination "never to be a victim again."

To say this another way, an intense negative focus eventually forms a boundary around the inner person—something like the thick, high stone walls of a prison. In fact, it is a spiritual prison from which the soul cannot see out. On the inside of this wall is scrawled, "An eye for an eye." It's the only truth we know; therefore, it must be the only truth there is.

For those of us who live inside these rigid walls, it's hard to envision, let alone to believe, that another realm of possibility lies beyond these walls and the single truth we repeat to ourselves, and it's impossible to believe there is any different way to resolve offenses when they occur. So it was for the teachers of the law when Jesus confronted them with a new possibility. The very concept of forgiveness was beyond them, just as it seems beyond us.

And so we come to a fifth trait of the individual who becomes stuck in a legalistic viewpoint: When the inner law we live by is not satisfied—when we perceive that justice is not done—*we cannot find rest for our souls.* The restless drive for justice can become consuming. In Victor Hugo's *Les Misérables,* Detective Javert seeks throughout his whole life to re-imprison Jean Valjean for the crime of stealing bread as a youth, even long after Valjean has become a great-hearted philanthropist. Javert is the embodiment of the restless legalist. This inability to rest can also cause us to develop a resentment toward God (after all, isn't He ultimately in charge of fairness and punishing wrongdoers?), and the longer the injustice stands the colder we feel toward Him.

The teachers of the law would no doubt join the psalmist in his many bitter cries: "How long, oh Lord? Why don't you bring justice?" "When will you defeat my enemies and bring them to shame?" "When will you kill the wicked?"

We use different language today, of course, and some of us are too respectful of God to confront Him directly with angry prayers—but the same resentful restlessness still exists. We find it buried in angry *self-talk* that we carry on when we're alone. It emerges in overreactions to people who are innocent of any offense, but whose words or actions remind us of the offender. It can haunt our dreams and daydreams, in which we envision the offender embarrassed, shamed, financially ruined, hurt, and even killed. These are all indications that, according to the unsatisfied laws of our innermost being, nothing but justice will do.

Unwittingly, we have laid the ultimate spiritual trap for ourselves.

WAITING FOR THE AX TO FALL

Finally, we come to the sixth trait of the legalistic spirit. It's a trait buried so deeply in most of us that we do not see it—or when we do, we don't recognize it for the deadly thing it is. *When we sin, or commit even a minor fault, our own demand to see justice makes it impossible to believe that we can be forgiven without suffering punishment. And so we are left living in uneasy anticipation, expecting God to wound or crush us for what we've done.* We have condemned ourselves, and we live every day "waiting for the ax to fall," to use a modern phrase.

In the eyes of the one who is in any degree subject to the legalistic spirit, it doesn't matter whether the offense is great or small. Nor does it matter how strongly the person insists she has been "forgiven" by God because she trusts in Jesus' atoning sacrifice on the cross. This self-condemning mindset is native in every one of us, and until it is confronted it will lie hidden within until some disturbance, some conflict with another, brings it out into the light of day.

David recently interviewed more than a dozen men who had participated in aborting unborn children. Later, these men consciously committed their lives to God, and insist they trust in Christ for redemption from their sins. Each one experiences a measure of peace. They express compassion for others who, out of fear, confusion, or despair, also choose abortion. And yet these same Christian men experienced a terrible anxiety during their wives' pregnancies and after the births of their present children, even if many years had passed since the abortion.

The guilty fear experienced by these men—and by all others who believe they have committed an "unpardonable sin"—is the fear of the *condemned*. It's the fear that God is just biding His time with them. Soon, life will bring them something they cherish— a child, a spouse, a possession, an occupation. And *then* God will deliver the blow that brings maximum pain by taking away what they love most. A parent who aborted a child might live in fear that God is going to punish him for ending the life of one precious child by harming or killing one of his now-living children. Even though the doctrines they believe, and the logical processes in their heads, tell them a God of mercy surely isn't like this, their hearts tell them otherwise. The anguish many of these people experience while they wait for their "sentence" to be meted out is agonizing and consuming.

Every one of us carries our own list of "unforgivable" sins for which we condemn ourselves. These correspond to a set of inner laws only we ourselves know. This list includes not only the obvious crimes against humanity we would never commit, but more common things that are "offenses" in our eyes—everything from simple social gaffes to greater "failures" in our relationships.

All his life, Cal lived by the inner law that *family comes first*. He often belittled and felt angry toward his sister, who, it seemed to him, most often let her commitment to friends come before family. When she failed to show up at family gatherings because she had "something more important to do," Cal judged her bitterly.

When Cal was in his late thirties, his mother was diagnosed with cancer. Doctors kept telling them she had "only weeks to live," but she lived on for months, experiencing many ups and downs. A period of rapid deterioration was followed by an amazing rally. Her situation was highly unpredictable. As the only son, Cal believed he should spend as much time at her bedside as possible. And he did so, given the demands of his own family and career. During this up-and-down period, however, his career demanded that he travel. It was unavoidable. Cal called his dad prior to one trip that would keep him away several days and accepted his father's assessment: "She's doing pretty well. She's eating, and she's in good spirits." With that assurance, he went on the business trip.

When Cal returned, he heard his wife and children crying as he carried his suitcase in the door. "Your father called five minutes ago. Your mom took a sudden turn for the worse just a few hours ago. She's gone."

Having broken his own inner law—*family comes first*—Cal bitterly railed against himself: "Why wasn't I there for Mom at the hour of her death? What kind of son am I?" To make things worse, a family member told him his mother had asked for him the morning of her death. To this day, he tells himself, "I deserve to die all alone somewhere . . . the way Mom died without seeing her only son again."

What's most notable about Cal's experience is that the condemnation he heaped on his sister for many years was turned back on him full force when he committed the "unpardonable sin" by breaking one of the most important laws he lived by.

And so it is for everyone who has written within, on the stony tablets of human hearts, laws that must not be broken. Because this includes every one of us, we all wind up in the same place— imprisoned by the legalistic spirit and its demands for punishment. Until we escape, we stand in need of both forgiving others and being forgiven ourselves. We live with what seems to be an unsatisfied hunger for justice, when in fact we are experiencing an unsatisfied hunger to be forgiven.

THE WAY OF ESCAPE

What we've just seen are the costs of unforgiveness—costs none of us can afford to pay because they mean forfeiting the peace, stability, and soundness of our inner being.

The question now is, How can we escape from the imprisonment of the legalistic spirit and the terrible costs we pay because of it? Can we experience the power of deep, satisfying forgiveness?

This is exactly where Jesus' impossible message, the soul-freeing way of the gospel, comes in:

"Forgive, and you will be forgiven" (Luke 6:37).

This is also the point at which we become hung up. We do so because most of us mistakenly believe that forgiveness must begin with a feeling that comes as naturally as, and in great enough measure to override, the old natural impulse to retaliate and seek punishment.

We say, "I wish I *could* forgive [the offender], but I don't *feel* very forgiving."

Or, "I wish I *could* forgive myself, but I don't *feel* like I'm forgiven."

Feelings are often downplayed in spiritual matters. What's

important, we're told, is that we "believe the right things"—
"Feelings are tricky and unreliable." There's truth in this, of
course. And yet we've seen how powerful life-controlling feelings,
especially buried feelings, can be.

Jesus undoubtedly knew that "feeling" either forgiving or forgiven is not natural to human beings, given our ingrained impulse
to seek revenge. He knew the rutted path that this natural impulse
had formed in our habits—our words, actions, *and* feelings.

It's our belief that Jesus' words, "Forgive, and you will be forgiven," lie at the heart of the gospel and hold the key to
experiencing incredible health and wellness, as well as peace with
God, with others, and with ourselves. We believe they lie at the
head of a new path for the soul, and that learning what these
words mean, and how to live them, will bring us to a profound
wholeness we have never imagined.

For that reason, we believe that every opportunity to forgive
is an opportunity to become more whole as human beings.

Let's consider now Jesus' path to wholeness and spiritual
maturity.

CHAPTER THREE

FORGIVE, AND YOU WILL BE FORGIVEN

IN THE PREVIOUS CHAPTER WE SAW WHAT HAPPENS WHEN WE do not counter the natural impulse to get revenge. We allow deep ruts to form within, in our habitual response to offenses. Soon our interior tendencies become so deeply ingrained that we essentially become imprisoned by them and see no other reasonable way to respond to offenses.

First, we tend to carry offenses inside us, even reliving them, until the offender has been "paid back" the offense in kind. This can be as simple as carrying a sense of "woundedness" because a friend has never said she was sorry for missing your birthday, or as intense as being plagued by dreams of finding and shooting the drunk driver who struck and killed your child and drove off.

Second, we tend to become focused on faultfinding and we bear down on the offender, seeing more and more shortcomings as time goes on.

Gradually, unforgiveness becomes aggressive within us, like a cancer in the spirit.

Third, we tend to become hypercritical. This can show itself in minor ways, like being oversensitive and reading offenses into comments and actions; or it can be as intense as spreading rumors and gossip or attempting to get others "on our side" against the offender.

Fourth, we develop a hardness, a tendency to be critical, callous, tough, unyielding—not only toward the original offender, but toward everyone. Our attitude is: "Play by *my* rules, or *pay*. And I'll tell you when you've paid enough."

Fifth, because offenses *will* continue to occur, and because others will inevitably *not* "pay enough" for their sins against us, our spirits become more restless and agitated. People are not fair; life is not fair; God is not fair. We become bitter because we don't see the justice we demand.

Finally, when we find ourselves in a fault or a sin, our souls condemn us. At some level of consciousness we live in guilty fear, believing God is just biding His time, waiting for us to come into possession of something we love so He can take it away in order to crush us as payback for our wrongs. What began as an attitude of holding grudges against others boomerangs and imprisons us in guilt and fear as we wait for God to drop the ax.

We believe this unhappy outcome of unforgiveness is what Jesus meant when He said, "Do not judge, or you too will be judged" (Matthew 7:1). Because Jesus came to "fulfill the law" (Matthew 5:17), He was not creating a new law for us to either obey or be displeasing to God. Rather, it seems He was warning us that when we try to imprison someone else in unforgiveness with a condemning, punishing attitude, we inevitably imprison, condemn, and punish *ourselves*.

Before we move on to examine the new and soul-freeing response Jesus came to teach, we need to look at two important factors that affect our ability to learn how to forgive.

FLEXIBILITY AND DISCERNMENT

In order to live healthy lives, every one of us needs to develop a *flexible response system*. This means simply that we need to have at our disposal various responses to life circumstances and other people. The problem is, many of us do not naturally possess this kind of flexibility in the face of a challenge.

Some of us learn mainly to feel hurt, rejected, and sad—a *retreating* response pattern that leads us toward depression. Others learn mainly to respond with anger and aggression—an *attacking* response pattern that leads us toward hostility. Still others learn mainly to avoid or ignore offenses—a *pretending* response pattern that leads toward indifference and aloofness. Most of us will tend toward one of these habits over the others.

We need to develop a full range of responses to the many life circumstances we encounter—including being offended. In plain language, there are indeed times to back off, hold our ground, and wait for an appropriate time and circumstance to confront an offender. There are also times when our response needs to be swift and firm in no uncertain terms in order to stop an offense from occurring again. While we don't need to jump on every offense, especially those of a minor nature, avoiding or ignoring chronic irritations or major offenses is not productive. The point is, overall, growing to maturity includes testing out these responses to see *when* they are appropriate, and *how* to use them. As we grow, we can even learn how to use our responses *not just for our own benefit, but for the benefit of the other parties involved.*

Second, we need to consider an unnecessary conflict in which many people find themselves. The conflict stems from a misunderstanding of Jesus' statement quoted earlier: "Do not judge, or you too will be judged." Many people believe this means we are never to notice that others are doing wrong, never notice they are hurting or offending us. When we think this way, we become caught in an interior conflict. We can't *help* but notice when someone is harming us or treating us badly, but we tell ourselves we shouldn't notice it. Noticing is not "the Christian thing to do." And so, unable to prevent ourselves from noticing, we judge ourselves to be "unChristian." Or, even if we're not that hard on ourselves, we interpret this as a "hard saying" of Jesus—an impossibility He dropped in our path intending to show us how weak and sinful and imperfect we are.

We can free ourselves from unnecessary conflict and guilt by making a simple but critical distinction: the distinction between *discernment* and *judgment.*

Discernment means simply that we perceive something that may not be entirely obvious. For instance, Bob's assistant managed to mention the "flagging numbers" in Bob's sales division during every meeting with the company chief financial officer. Her negative comments also colored meetings with his sales staff. When Bob confronted her, she denied malicious intent, but after several confrontations she admitted she thought she could do a far better job. Bob correctly discerned she was after his position. When she continued to undermine him, he let her go.

To *judge,* on the other hand, means to assign someone to an ultimate destiny or to believe that person will never, can never, change. Judging attitudes and statements can be directed at individuals: "You'll never amount to anything." "You'll never change." "You're nothing but a [liar, thief, fool, and so on], and you always will be." Or they can be directed at whole groups: "You can't trust [women, men]." "Everyone who belongs to [a certain group] is beyond help." A judging attitude says a person is *condemned* to stay a certain way forever, and so there's no need to interact with him; punishment or exclusion is thought to be the only right way to deal with the individual.

Jesus did indeed tell us not to judge—meaning that we are not to dismiss people out of hand, or to think of them as beyond the capacity to change, or to believe we know their eternal destiny. We *discern* in order to keep from being victimized, but we are not to *judge.*

This brings us back to our main point: We do not judge because judgment—like its counterpart, unforgiveness—prevents us from developing the flexible response system we need both for our own interior benefit and the potential good of others. If we judge, we create in ourselves a *legalistic spirit* and we wind up, as Jesus warned, living in an interior climate that knows only a dull, tormenting sense of condemnation.

FORGIVE, AND YOU UNDERSTAND FORGIVENESS

As we have learned, the legalistic mind can hear Jesus' statement "Forgive, and you will be forgiven" and perceive it only as a binding law.

But here is the wonderful truth, the hope of the gospel: When we turn our lives over to God and begin to live in accordance with His directives, *we are totally forgiven no matter how imperfectly we forgive others.* We are all on an uneven march, sometimes limping and lurching, other times leaping, toward spiritual wholeness and maturity. We can cripple ourselves in this process by noticing every time we don't *feel* forgiving, telling ourselves we're no good at this spiritual growth stuff and that we'll never make it.

When Jesus said, "Forgive, and you will be forgiven," we believe He was speaking about the process of learning to forgive — which ultimately produces a constant experience of a deep, powerful sense that we are forgiven. Just as judging leads to *wrongly* perceiving we are judged and condemned by God, forgiving leads to *correctly* perceiving His wonderful, restful forgiveness.

The process of forgiveness begins when we start to practice a new impulse in response to offenses. That is the *impulse to keep ourselves free from the potentially soul-trapping impulse to seek revenge.* In an imperfect world, where injustice and unfairness often win out, forgiveness is the starting point of both sanity and spiritual freedom.

Yes, you've read this correctly. Developing a spirit of forgiveness starts when we know that forgiveness is in *our own* best interest.

Later on, the practice of forgiveness is likely to generate another desire — *the genuine desire to see the offending person change and set out on a relationally, spiritually healthy new path.* To our own amazement, we actually forgive as a means of showing the way to a better kind of living.

Writing this, we know that some resist and reject the idea of helping the offender, labeling it a "codependent" urge. *Codependence,* while generally a useful term, is frequently misused today because it's been stretched far beyond its actual meaning. Codependence refers to a state in which one *cannot* experience peace and settledness within until someone else experiences these things too, because one feels responsible to help produce peace and happiness or good behavior in another. Unforgiveness leaves us in a negative version of codependence, in the sense of assuming responsibility to make the offender experience anguish and grief. Forgiveness sets us entirely free to go on, whether or not the offender experiences these things or changes one iota for the better.

And yet the desire to see the offender changed, set free from past behaviors, *will* arise in the forgiving soul. When we know the power of forgiveness, we want to tell other people, "There is something more, something greater, than living with hurt, anger, and the drive to get retribution. You've *got* to experience what forgiveness will do. You won't believe how good it is."

But the question remains: *How* do we learn to forgive, so that we can experience the deep soul-rest of forgiveness Jesus promises?

Forgiveness, like all true lessons of the soul, is only learned in the school of real life. We can read books and hear messages, but then we're only learning about forgiveness at the limited level of the intellect. Lessons of the soul must be learned by *feel*. Perhaps an analogy from our physical experience will help.

Let's say that you want to learn how to play golf. You may buy golfing magazines and instructional videos to teach you some basics before stepping up to the tee. But ultimately, the only way to learn how to golf is to get out on a course and learn what it feels like to swing and connect with the ball, what force is required to drive down the fairway, and what is the right touch to use to sink a putt from various distances. This is known as *kinesthetic learning,* which means to learn by feeling. The knowledge of how to play golf centers itself not just in the brain, but in nerves and muscles throughout the body.

Learning to forgive is similar in that it is a process in which we are retraining our core reactions—our spiritual nerve impulses, if you will—how to respond in the new, soul-freeing, self-benefiting way we're being shown. Because we're completely forgiven, and not being judged by God for our early faltering efforts, we're as free as the new golfer to set out and try our hand at forgiving, knowing our early efforts are likely to be imperfect. In fact, we're likely to experience a mixture of feelings at first—a 50-50 mix of the old desire to punish and the new desire to erase the debt.

Imperfection is not failure. Like learning to golf, learning to forgive major and chronic offenses takes time as a new habit path is formed in our innermost being. At the beginning, we help ourselves along tremendously by walking slowly through the process the way we might, again, go through a golf swing in slow motion to concentrate and become aware of what every part of that motion feels like. It can help to do this together here.

Call to mind a particular offense, perhaps something you've held against another for a long time or with some intensity. Let yourself really feel the anger, sadness, or disappointment the offense caused you. Take time to notice changes in your breathing, heart rate, or muscle tension.

At this point, it's important to understand the power at your disposal—that is, *the power to recreate a spiritual, emotional, and physical state of being by directing your focus.* This is not turning Christian spirituality into a mind science—it is merely slowing down a lightning-fast reaction we had heretofore been unable to change in order to understand our part in transforming it.

We can recognize our part in transforming our spiritual core responses by understanding another of Jesus' important state-ments: "If you forgive anyone his sins, they are forgiven; if you do not forgive them, they are not forgiven" (John 20:23). Saying this, Jesus reminded His disciples of a truth He demonstrated for them some time before, when He healed the paralyzed man— though the power to decide eternal destinies lies only with God, the "authority *on earth* to forgive sins" lies with us mortals (Matthew 9:6,8, emphasis added).

Whatever granting us "the authority to forgive sins" may mean in various branches of the Christian church, we believe it has a practical meaning of utmost importance: Just as we have the power to focus intensely on our anger and sadness and impulse to revenge, we have an even greater power that comes from *refocusing our attention on the way it feels to know we are forgiven.* This is the power, or "authority," to create a new spiritual, emo-tional, and physical state of being that is defined by peace, restfulness, and the ability to freely let go of offenses.

We have the keys to our own inner prison because we have the power to be free from within, whether or not an offender is made to suffer punishment. We have the ability to offer offenders a new possibility, a way to get out of the cycle of hurt and fear of retribution. We have the authority, by offering forgiveness, to help them examine the wrongs they do and begin to live in a new way.

BUT THIS IS THE "REAL WORLD"

Many today ask, Is forgiveness realistic? What *good* does forgive-ness do? And what if the offender has done something so wrong, so hurtful, that it cannot be "simply forgiven"? Wouldn't society fall into lawless anarchy if criminals were not held responsible for their crimes?

We suspect that people who insist on having answers to such questions are prisoners to a desired outcome in greater measure than they know. They would *like* to know that their words and actions will control the actions of another and get them what they want sooner or later. These people have missed the point: *We do not have the power to control others' actions, and we cannot make them feel remorseful or in need of making soul-restoring recompense for what they've done wrong.* This lies beyond our authority.

"Simple forgiveness" is for all those little infractions of life—forgotten anniversaries, thoughtless remarks, and the carelessness that caused spilled milk. In cases where a serious offense has been committed, or a habit of offense has seated itself in someone, forgiveness has to be offered in combination with other responses.

As men and women on the road to maturity, we have to accept that all people are a mixture, and that many situations will require us to mix forgiveness with some other response as well. "Simple forgiveness" will not do. The best chance for "good" to occur will come from learning to balance several impulses at once.

This is not quite as complicated as it sounds. In fact, every one of us experiences complicated feelings. What we need is a way to sort them out and prioritize them. Choosing to forgive does this for us—even when terrible offenses occur.

Cheryl's story will help to illustrate what forgiveness in the "real world" can be like.

Cheryl's brother was brutally murdered, and there seemed ample evidence to convict the man accused. Tragically, the key witness, who'd heard the accused admit to the crime, was killed accidentally before his testimony had been recorded. The murderer got off scot-free.

Cheryl's mother plummeted into endless, debilitating rounds of grief, anger, and depression, while her father dropped out of life, burying himself in isolating pastimes and trivial hobbies. At first Cheryl was in despair. But with the help of a counselor she chose to forgive the murderer, even though her brother was dead and his killer was living as a free man. But canceling the debt allowed Cheryl to move through grief and anger. She refocused her life around the future—growing in intimacy with her husband, loving and enjoying her children, even learning how to empathize with and relate to her parents in their impaired state. In short, when the outcome of the trial was not in her favor, Cheryl chose to be flexible and find another way to *do life* without the immediate justice she'd hoped for.

One of the things that got Cheryl through was certainly the development of a faith that includes a view that eternal justice will be done someday. In a sense, "delaying gratification" of her desire to see justice is part of her flexible response system. She says, "I've had faith all my life. But when my brother's killer went free I was forced to expand my view of life and God. Quite honestly, my belief in a God who holds justice in His hand was paper-thin before. Now it's a concept that's rich and alive for me. It's not only changed the way I look at my situation, but it's opened my eyes to the struggles of the poor and minorities. It's enriched and broadened my life in ways I could never have imagined."

We'll look more at belief in a "greater justice" in a later chapter. For now, let's stick with Cheryl's story for a moment, because there's a bit more to it.

A dozen years after her brother's murder, an investigator came across some new evidence that could link the accused man to the crime. A new trial was granted. Cheryl's mother was pitched into racking bouts of grief and anger, and was diagnosed with manic-depressive disorder. Her father, in Cheryl's words, "just fell apart." Unable to face the anguish of another trial—seeing old pictures of his son's corpse, reliving those terrible days—he left Cheryl's mother and went to live with a brother out-of-state. A month later he filed for divorce.

It would be wonderful to say the murderer was convicted in the second trial. Unfortunately, the new evidence did not convince the jury. And yet—even with new injuries added to old—Cheryl held tightly to her conviction that forgiveness was her best choice, the healthiest way through all these painful and destructive circumstances.

"The prosecutor told me at the outset there was a 50-50 chance for conviction," says Cheryl. "I decided I didn't want to rest my inner well-being on those or any other odds. I didn't want to base my well-being on circumstances at all. If there's one thing life has taught me, it's that circumstances can go from wonderful to hellish in a moment of time. I have to base my life on something more steady than that.

"Because I've made the choice to forgive, I felt buoyed by an incredible peace through the whole ordeal of the second trial. And even before that, I was strong and steady, and able to help the prosecutor and investigators assemble the best case possible. I know I couldn't have contributed much to their efforts if I'd been wiped out by grief and anger, and not steady in my thinking."

And the story is not all told.

Leaving the courtroom after the "not guilty" verdict, Cheryl stepped into the hallway—only to find herself face to face with the accused, his wife, and his attorney, celebrating his victory. For a moment, everyone froze. The prosecutor tried to gently usher Cheryl away, but something in her said she could not pass up a chance that would never come again.

Her eyes met the eyes of her brother's killer. "You need to know two things," Cheryl said evenly. She was feeling the sting of losing the trial, yet she'd made a choice of which path she wanted to follow. "First, because I believe you committed a crime, I've had to do everything I could to see justice done.

"That doesn't change the second thing you need to know. I don't know why you killed my brother that night, but whatever your reasons were, I forgive you. I don't wish any evil on you. I hope you'll come to peace in yourself."

Even as Cheryl was speaking, the man's wife was pulling at his arm, trying to interrupt.

"But when I said, 'I forgive you, I don't wish you evil,' it was like seeing someone get hit by a lightning bolt," says Cheryl. "Who can say? Maybe he'll remember my words, and someday when guilt is tearing him apart he'll finally confess. Maybe not.

"I only know telling him he's forgiven did *me* a world of good. It kept my head straight, and allowed me to stay calm and focused during the new investigation and trial. And in spite of all the destruction to my original family, I'm able to go on and live a great life with my husband and children."

People ask her *how* she can forgive, and Cheryl replies, "I don't know how to explain it exactly. In the beginning I struggled, of course. Then I came to the logical conclusion that forgiveness was better than bitterness. At first, saying I forgave my brother's killer was kind of mechanical. But then something changed.

"Once I was having a bad morning, and I said some terrible things to my kids while I was sending them off to school. In fact, I'd been hard on them for a whole week. I knew I had to wait the whole day to tell them how sorry I was, to explain myself and ask forgiveness. In my mind's eye I could imagine them looking at me, and knew they didn't even need an explanation. Because kids love their moms and dads so much, they don't even need to hear you say why you're sorry. They're just so happy your heart has changed.

"That got me thinking about God, and how quick and free His forgiveness is. It seemed to me that saying 'I'm sorry' is more for *our* benefit because it means we've seen what we've done wrong. I thought how difficult it would be to say 'sorry' to my kids, or to God, if I knew they would face me with hard looks and if I knew they were going to make me pay somehow for my meanness. But they don't. They're just relieved that I've come to my senses. It's *grace*. And grace gives you the freedom to relax and look inside yourself to understand why you do the nasty things you sometimes do. That's when you can change.

"Somewhere in all this, waiting for my kids to come home, I experienced this overwhelming sense of forgiveness at a very deep level. I felt . . . *free*. Like every time I make a mistake, God was saying, 'Okay, you've hurt someone. But instead of just feeling guilty and not facing it, I want you to think about *why* you're doing what you're doing. Then come to Me and we'll come up with a better, healthier way that doesn't hurt anyone.'

"And then the tears came," Cheryl confides. "I hadn't been thinking of him at all—but I suddenly thought of my brother's killer. I knew that if I wanted to continue experiencing this forgiveness—I guess you'd call it a *state of grace*—I had to offer forgiveness to him, too. Sort of 'use it or lose it.'

"That's when it made sense to me. 'Forgive, and you will be forgiven.' It's a great system, when you think about it."

BRINGING FORGIVENESS INTO YOUR WORLD

Cheryl recognized the true authority she had at her disposal—the power to add to the terrible damage done to her family, or to set herself on a new path into the future, and even to offer this same possibility to her offender. By replacing judgment and condemnation with forgiveness, she also experienced a profound sense of God's forgiveness, which has given her strength and peace to walk through a great and ongoing tragedy without being personally ruined.

Do you want this same chance for yourself? And your future? It is the chance to begin all over. Not begin where you were before, because the harm and loss has changed that world for you forever. But it is the chance, by introducing forgiveness, to begin as a new person whose life is not under the dictate of circumstances . . . to cooperate with God in directing the course of your life, and maybe the lives of others, to new and better ends.

Lori and Kevin, whom we met in the first chapter, offered themselves and each other that chance. Working together, they are creating a new life for themselves, one they never thought possible.

Consider what each has to say about the power of forgiveness.

Lori

Forgiving my husband was not an easy task—possibly it was the hardest thing I've ever done.

In the first part of our marriage, when Kevin hurt me, I just thought I had to protect myself at all costs. Forgiveness was simply not an option.

I really didn't know what it meant. I just knew that when Kevin hurt me, I was hurt and angry. That's a natural response. But then, without knowing it, somewhere inside I made the decision to hang on to hurt and anger. Like all of us, I began to use these emotions as a protective wall, believing they'd keep me safe from any more damage. It seemed to work. It kept other people away. But after awhile hurt and anger is all you feel, all you can see whenever you look at any person who hurts you.

What I didn't realize is that using these emotions to protect yourself doesn't really work. You keep getting hurt anyway. And besides that, it gets easier and easier to hold on to negative emotions, harder and harder to let them go and feel positive emotions.

In time, I realized that anger and hurt were not protecting me—they were beginning to smother me. By not forgiving, I was as stuck as if I was at the bottom of a deep, dark well with no way out. I realized I'd dug this pit myself by developing a *habit* of dwelling on hurts. Instead of learning how to grow beyond hurt and anger, I'd sunk right into the middle of it. By holding a grudge, I'd always live my life looking back. I'd never move forward.

I had to decide that I wanted to thrive and grow. I had to ask myself how I was going to do that spiritually and emotionally if I stayed stuck, rehearsing the pain people had caused me. *The plain truth is that unless you forgive, you cannot grow.*

So I was faced with a choice: I could stay angry and

hurt . . . and very stuck. Or I could forgive my husband and move forward with a fresh new start.

But there was an enormous hurdle for me.

To me, forgiveness meant *surrender*—giving up the payback I felt I was owed. To me, surrendering meant to bow down, to give up an important part of myself. It meant letting down the emotional barriers I'd put up, and that meant leaving my soul completely exposed. Because of the way I was thinking, to me, surrendering to forgiveness also meant *losing*. I was raised to never surrender, to never lose!

So as I faced my choices, holding on to anger and hurt felt like the right thing. Forgiveness felt like nothing but a huge gamble. And the thing I was gambling was my own soul—which is a very high-stakes thing to wager!

In the end I chose to forgive. As hard as it was for me to stand there with my naked soul, though, I can tell you it has been worth it. It was like a miracle to feel old layers of hurt and anger fall away, to feel free and whole.

I didn't know then what I know now—that to forgive is actually to win.

For Kevin, experiencing Lori's forgiveness was somewhat revolutionary as well. In the past, when she'd blamed and attacked him for his failures, he'd recoiled defensively and refused to look at the effect of his actions on her. When forgiveness drained the negative emotional charge from the atmosphere of their relationship, it was easier for them to talk (certainly not without emotion) about what his boyish immaturity caused him to do and why it was still there in a man's body.

Through this healing dialogue, Kevin was able to look honestly at himself. He was able to forgive himself—deep inside, he'd known all along he was acting in immature ways but had been too ashamed to face it. He realized for the first time that he *had* to take responsibility for his words and actions in their relationship. He realized that in every relationship, refusing to take responsibility for yourself and what you do is simply not an option. Within this new atmosphere of forgiveness, though, he knew that he was now free to make mistakes on his personal road to maturity and, with Lori's help, to learn from them.

Here's what he has to say.

Kevin

In order to make my relationship with Lori work, I had to learn to forgive myself.

This was not an easy thing to get a handle on, considering the fact that I'd made so many mistakes in our marriage.

At first, I wanted to go back to my old habit. I wanted to blame her for noticing everything that was wrong. For years, I'd defended myself by thinking everything wrong with our relationship was really her fault, or just in her imagination. No way would I let myself admit I did all the things she claimed—like not communicating, not showing her respect, and not showing any emotion one way or the other. I frustrated her attempts to talk about these things, and brushed her off by saying, "What are you talking about?"

It is so much easier to blame someone else instead of yourself.

When our marriage was in crisis, I knew that I did not want to lose what we had made together. Ultimately, to do that, I had to take a good hard look at myself and realize that maybe there was some truth in what she said. Looking back, I can remember her telling me these things, and completely not hearing her at all.

Then it dawned on me that I was the one to blame for these things. Not an easy thing to do. So I had to take responsibility for my faults and ultimately grow up. By taking responsibility I did not have her to blame anymore—

only myself. That was when I had to learn to forgive myself. Knowing what I would be missing in my life if I did not forgive myself was incentive enough to do the work this requires.

First, I had to look deep inside and realize that I was willing to change the things that needed to be changed. I also had to accept that, just as all people make mistakes, I was making mistakes. I had to think through why I'd stubbornly held on to the attitudes and ways I related to Lori for so long. When I was able to understand myself, I was also able to see that there were other ways to get to the things I wanted—and that meant relating, talking, working things out together, which was what Lori had been trying to get across to me for years.

In the end, I was able to forgive myself. Understanding helped me with forgiveness.

With great effort—the supernatural effort it requires to live above our old impulse to revenge—both Lori and Kevin were able to give up resentment, anger, and strong urges to make the other pay back an emotional debt. As their trust grew and their love was restored, it became easier with time to cancel all the old debts. Today, they enjoy a better marriage than before, partly due to the pain they have survived together—but mostly because they are now, finally, willing to offer forgiveness *freely* to each other.

Whatever your situation, we want you to know it is possible to bring forgiveness into your world, and to allow its transforming power a chance to work. Knowing we have this authority at our disposal, it becomes our responsibility to choose.

Perhaps it's time to ask yourself:

What will I win by holding on to the hurt, anger, and sadness that go along with unforgiveness? What will I really lose by forgiving?

Only you can answer these questions.

CHAPTER FOUR

WHAT FORGIVENESS IS NOT

FORGIVENESS—AS A LIFE HABIT—IS NOT EASY. JUST when you think you've mastered it in one part of your life, or in one relationship, some new offense touches a deeply treasured piece of you, and the hurt and anger flare again.

Sometimes our impulse to judge and see retribution arises when we hear about sad or terrible things done to other people. Consider these two tragic stories.

Ginger, a thirty-five-year-old woman with a great personality, suffered lifelong depression.

Her troubles began when she was a teenager who felt socially inept. Her parents were rigid in their rules, thinking their incredibly high standards would make their bright, attractive child the best among her peers. The trouble was, Ginger could never be quite good enough.

When Ginger's youth pastor, Len, began to pay special attention to her, she responded with gratitude. It felt good to be noticed by a man she respected and liked, and they developed a special friendship. Len and his wife, Judy, invited her to their home and even took her on trips with them. Ginger's parents were appreciative, and condoned the relationship. They saw their shy, self-conscious daughter become more at ease socially.

After some months, though, her parents thought Ginger seemed to regress a bit. She became secretive and a little withdrawn, but they attributed this to her age. They were so glad for the kindness Len and Judy were offering to their child.

One day, however, Ginger's father happened across a letter from Len. As he read it, he felt uneasy. Something about it implied a bit more than a pastoral interest in a shy teenager.

He promptly cut off all contact between Ginger and Len — but the damage had been done.

Somewhere along the line, Len — a representative of God — had seduced this innocent young woman. He robbed her of her innocence and touched off incredible self-loathing in her that pitched her into decades of depression and struggle.

By the time she was in her mid-thirties, Ginger was horribly confused. She wanted to see Len punished, but he was long gone and she didn't have the emotional energy to search for him. She no longer knew who to trust. She doubted herself in all relationships and believed that other people only liked her for what she could do, not for who she was. Such was the legacy left by her parents' well-meaning but overbearing moral demands, coupled with Len's selfishness and betrayal. Along with the depression, Ginger held deep doubts about the Christian faith and about God.

Ginger has been left with a scarred spirit and a marred past.

Ian was the youngest of three handsome brothers. The older two were good at sports and intellectually successful, too. Ian, though good-looking and smart like his brothers, suffered from a congenital deformity of his feet. The toes of both feet turned noticeably inward, making it so difficult for him to walk that he sometimes tripped over his own feet. It was impossible for him to run. Sports, which he loved, were not an option.

At the time Ian was very young, Grace was practicing pediatrics. Even then she could see he felt out of it. He looked depressed and could not compete with his brothers or peers. A very simple surgical procedure would correct his feet and open a new world of options to him.

Yet when Grace tried to refer this precious little boy to a fine orthopedic physician, Ian's father refused. At first, she thought she'd failed to hear him correctly, so she asked him to repeat himself.

"I told you no child of mine is *defective*—which is what you're implying."

"I'm very sorry," Grace stammered. "I didn't mean that at all. I only meant that a simple surgery will make it possible for Ian . . ."

"When Ian wants to, he can walk the right way," he interrupted. "He'll grow out of it, if he does what I tell him."

Ian's life was an ongoing nightmare. At his father's command, Ian could make a heroic effort to walk with his feet appearing straight. But time and conscious effort would not correct the formation of his bones. Because of his father's pride or insecurity, the boy was left to struggle through life, trying to compensate for his embarrassing awkwardness. By the time he reached adulthood, surgical correction would not work. Small wonder he later developed serious phobias. He was angry at the man he so needed, and bitter he'd been needlessly deprived of a normal life.

Hearing tragedies like these—and worse—is it any wonder most of the world believes forgiveness is a lot of religious foolishness? Because it's so commonly held that forgiveness is *not* the healthy answer to hurts, we should take a look at what some of today's "experts" are touting.

THE WORLD'S RESPONSE TO HURT

Not long ago, Dr. Susan Forward and her coauthor Craig Buck published a popular book called *Toxic Parents: Overcoming Their Hurtful Legacy and Reclaiming Your Life*. In no uncertain terms, Dr. Forward stated that we do not have to forgive parents—or, by implication, anyone else—who has hurt us. She insists that to forgive is actually wrong because it condones another's wrongdoing.

With "experts" publishing books like this, it's no surprise the general population believes that assigning blame and making it your goal to hold people accountable is the healthiest thing you can do for yourself.

Several years ago, Grace discussed her beliefs about forgiveness from a clinical standpoint at a public seminar for Christian counselors. Because it was known that she was speaking out of personal experience—a deep betrayal in an intimate relationship, and a painful public humiliation in the media—a reporter for a large-city newspaper attended in the interest of writing an article on the lecture. Grace spoke about the nightmare of this experience and the personal trauma, and then told about the costs and rewards of forgiving. When the writer approached her afterward, Grace was led to believe that an article would teach many people about the value and benefits of forgiving, so she agreed to work with her.

After talking to others the woman had interviewed to develop the piece, Grace discovered that the reporter was focused on ridiculing her and tearing apart her position on forgiveness.

When the article appeared, it was clear this reporter, like most of the world, believed Grace should seek revenge. "Some wrongs should never be forgiven," she wrote, then implied that Grace was everything from stupid to "codependent" to have forgiven the serious offenses she forgave. Sadly, this woman (and many others like her) do not have the first inkling about the profound power of forgiveness. Fortunately, the article was never published.

We surely must do our part in choosing to make ourselves open and ready to forgive and not count others' offenses against them. But there is also a greater power at work—the power of God's *grace.*

Grace is that unusual force that makes such spiritual actions as *forgiveness* real in us—the power that impresses it into our very being so that we know it in our core. Grace "makes the inner

light come on," as it did in Cheryl's case. It's the power that transforms an idea in our heads into a drive we know we must live by.

Grace is the transforming touch of God Himself.

This is why it's imperative to be growing in a relationship
with God if we want to grow in spiritual and psychological
health. When God created us He took the greatest risk possible,
giving us the power to choose—and we cannot downplay or dis-
count an individual's power to choose how he or she will focus
inner energies. But we also know that it is God's empowering
grace that joins with our choosing and, ultimately, makes living
a life of forgiveness possible—that and nothing else.

It's no wonder, then, that those who do not include a living,
active faith in their worldview also fail to understand the vast
importance and power of forgiveness. In the end, even as an exercise in good mental health, it does not make sense. Forgiveness
moves us beyond the boundaries of our humanity, into the realm
of faith and of God.

MOVING BEYOND THE BOUNDARIES

In order to move beyond the limitations imposed on forgiveness,
then, we can help ourselves along by clearing up misunderstandings. We need to understand what forgiveness is *not*.

First, forgiveness does not mean we will easily forget.

Roy wanted to resolve the conflicts that were destroying his marriage. He would forgive his wife's damaging attacks—but his
memory would haunt him, replaying the nasty confrontations. As he
turned the words and images over and over in his mind, he would
physically tense up until the physiological feeling of hurt was real
again, too. He literally *relived* the hurt and reinforced the memory.
Reopening his wounds in this way left him with fresh hurt and anger,
and a subtle remark by his wife triggered a burst of vengeful words.
And so the marriage was kept on edge, and not healed.

When you choose to forgive, you are also choosing to keep your mind free from the episode most of the time.

The power of our internal meditations is great, and, as Roy's experience shows, it triggers even physiological responses in us—and it digs the rut created by the old impulse to revenge even deeper.

Choosing to forget requires us to gently push aside the hurtful words and images and focus our thoughts on something else. This we can do, this we *must* do, until our mind is calmly fixed on forward-looking, not backward-looking ideas—such as life lessons learned from the incident. In this way, we reach the point where we are so free from memories that we all but forget what we have forgiven because our thought processes have moved on. At that point, the hurtful episode is truly in the past, and we remember only the lessons we have learned.

Second, forgiveness does not mean that you will allow anyone to wrong you over and over or allow others to commit the same offense.

To forgive, and to grow as a Christian, does not require acting as a doormat on which people can freely wipe their dirty feet. We are not "worms," though unfortunately some well-meaning Christians believe that we *are* as low as worms. (Sometimes we *feel* that way, but it's not so.) They take this idea from Scriptures such as Psalm 22:6, in which David writes, "But I am a worm and not a man, scorned by men and despised by the people." If you've been repeatedly abused over time, you'll empathize with David's feeling. But it is just a feeling, and not a fact. Believing we are "worms" in the eyes of God, and therefore it's okay for us to be treated like worms by others, is poor theology, and terribly destructive to the inner being.

Because we are men and women created in the image of God, Jesus restored to us the authority to forgive the sins and faults of others here on earth. Once we understand our true position in the eyes of God as sons and daughters, sharing in His work of healing and restoring the world, we understand that it is also important *not* to assume a false humility and say, "It doesn't matter that I was hurt. I'm not worth much anyway." We recognize why the imperative "Forgive!" means that we must stand up the moment after we have been victimized and, in spirit, become the *victor.*

In practical, everyday terms, this means we must take on the task of learning how to set strong, healthy boundaries. Practice will teach us just how far an offender can go before we—or the authorities—set limits on his or her actions.

Which brings us to the third point: Forgiveness does not mean that we condone or rationalize offenses.

Sandie is an example of someone who had to learn the balance that must exist between forgiving and setting firm boundaries.

Over most of her early years, Sandie had become the family scapegoat. If the dusting wasn't finished, Sandie was scolded. If her little brother hit her, *she* was obviously to blame. Even the church leaders learned, at her parents' request, how to lecture her in an effort to make her perfect. They couldn't see that she was a loving, upbeat, normal child, and only picked at her faults.

Even as an adult Sandie felt that when there was a problem it must somehow be her fault. She went to great lengths to be certain she hadn't "goofed," often making matters worse by her nearly paranoid fears. She could no longer tell where the lines of responsibility fell.

With help, Sandie learned how to determine whether she was indeed responsible for a problem or whether her family (and those who resembled family members) was again making her the scapegoat. Forgiving helped her walk free from the past hurts these people had heaped on her. And, just as great, her knowledge prevented further hurt. If she was at fault, she corrected her errors. If not, she was able to point out the facts to her accuser and to hand back responsibility. If the other party was willing, the two could then calmly work out the problem. If not, Sandie could walk away and put it behind her.

To do what Sandie has done is to balance forgiveness with the necessary skill of setting internal boundaries.

To take this a step further, consider how Sandie learned to establish boundaries—even when others were aggressive in their pressure and accusations.

Sandie began by telling her parents that she believed they'd been too critical of her and had passed on blame that she didn't deserve, and that it had injured her. She told them that far from wanting to cut them out of her life, she wanted to forgive and build a new, healthier relationship. "That means," she said, "if I begin to feel you're being unfairly critical of me, I'll have to stop the conversation until we can sort it out without blame being involved."

In her very next phone call, Sandie's mother began to launch a barrage. Sandie interrupted her, saying, "Mom—remember what I talked to you about last week? Sorry, I'm going to hang up now. I'll call you later when you've had a chance to think about it."

Not long after, in a personal confrontation initiated by her father, Sandie politely but firmly interrupted. "Dad—remember how I told you I would no longer listen to these unfair accusations? I'm going to run an errand now. If there's anything I can get for you while I'm out I'd be happy to, but I'm going to leave until we can talk without you blaming me."

You can see she was not retaliating, nor was she playing the victim. She had learned the important skill of setting boundaries.

We must also tell you honestly that no matter how respectfully Sandie spoke, her parents became furious. They yelled and became even *more* accusing. But Sandie stayed the course. It took time, but eventually her parents' old "game" was finished, and they saw that Sandie was trying to teach them a new and healthy way to interact. Forgiveness, and the calm strength it gave Sandie, overcame judgment and the harm it caused.

Why is setting boundaries an important counterbalance to forgiveness? Because boundary setting makes us firm, even as forgiving makes us graceful.

Fourth, forgiving does not mean that your offender will imme-diately see his or her error and change.

In fact, the one who offends you may never change at all. This is a possibility we have to allow for. To make someone change is not in your power; therefore, it's also not your responsibility. God alone can effect the transformation of another.

Too many times we're unwilling to forgive because we're not sure it will guarantee the kind of change we want, even demand, to see in the offender. We believe that holding anger, disapproval, and rejection over someone's head will force a change.

Not so.

Long ago Grace learned a lesson worth its weight in gold. She says, "I learned to give nothing away until I could give it freely—even if I never received any recognition or appreciation for giving it." This is the way we need to be with giving our forgiveness. We do it freely because it's for *our* good, not because we expect certain returns on it.

Forgiving, as we noted before, does *not* mean that we condone an offense. Wrongdoing can never be excused. We've seen the emotional wounds inflicted in the lives of too many people ever to take offense lightly. Jesus Himself said that whoever hurt another "would be better off thrown into the sea with a millstone around his [or her] neck. . . . In the nature of things there must be pitfalls, yet alas for the man who is responsible for them" (Matthew 18:6-7, PH). A penalty awaits those who intentionally wrong others and refuse to change.

Our job, through forgiving, is to establish a climate conducive to helping the offender learn crucial life lessons about goodness, love, and respect. And in the real world, this can take a lifetime.

Fifth, to be forgiving is not the same as being codependent.

We spoke to this misunderstanding in the last chapter, but return to it here for emphasis.

Codependency is a state in which one believes that his or her actions determine the emotional well-being or the future of another. While it's true that we all influence each other for good or ill, we are each ultimately responsible for our own attitudes, beliefs, choices, words, and actions.

If you've been following closely to this point, you can see clearly that forgiving, as we believe Jesus meant it, *sets us personally, entirely free.* We're set free, first, to make better, healthier choices in relation to the offender, and second, to free the offender to take responsibility (or not take it) for his or her own actions.

What we've been describing is the aspect of forgiveness that helps us to *let go* of an offense. There will be more to say later about this surprising side of forgiveness. But for now, we want you to clearly understand how forgiveness resolves an offense by letting it go.

LETTING GO

Because letting go of an offense is hard for many of us, it can be useful to look at it in five parts. Understanding the process will help in the long run.

1. Admit the pain.
Offenses always cause pain. It's only our pride that makes us deny it. Some take an attitude that says, "Who cares? You're insignificant in my life. You can't hurt me!" This insulates us from the acute pain of the moment, but it allows the infectious agent of resentment, like a toxic bacteria, to enter our soul. There it festers, creating the spiritual disease of bitterness. Such a condition gradually estranges us from others, from God, and even from ourselves as we become out of touch with our true inner state.

The truth is, whenever we love or like someone, we have hopes and expectations, and we give that person some measure of power to hurt us. The person may or may not exert that power, but it is there. It's an inescapable law of human relationships. What we're learning, by studying the way of forgiveness, is that we don't have to give others power to destroy us.

Denying pain keeps us from starting on the path to forgiveness. But the degree of pain required in this exercise is bearable. Honestly experiencing it long enough to understand the exact nature of the offense is actually the beginning of healing.

2. Work through confused feelings.

When an offense has occurred, we often need to work our way through a *zone of confusion*—a stage in which we must clearly, carefully sort out responsibilities in a particular incident.

When Grace was in her early years of training, she was privileged to hear a lecture by the well-known sociologist Virginia Satir. Satir taught that as children, we believe the world revolves around us. Although this tendency is strongest in our formative years, it also persists somewhat into adulthood. When traumatic events occur, kids will believe it's mostly their fault. ("If I hadn't made Dad angry he wouldn't have had a heart attack and died . . ." or ". . . slapped me around.") As adults we need to develop firm ground within ourselves on which to stand when we face an offender with the facts about his harmful words and actions.

This is what Sandie learned to do, as she set boundaries and learned to speak up for herself when her limits were violated.

3. Seek information.

Once we're beyond this zone of confusion and we're very clear as to the other's responsibility, we can help ourselves along by taking the next step: to seek information that tells us why the offender hurt us.

Gathering information is important because it takes us a step away from dwelling single-mindedly on how we were hurt or how we wish to see the other punished. It gives us a bit of distance. In our quest for understanding we may need to ask others, such as friends or family members, for information. If that's not possible or realistic, we can use our own imagination and place ourselves in the offender's position.

Remember, gathering information is not the same as looking for an excuse. No reasoning can excuse, for example, crimes against humanity such as torture, rape, extortion, blackmail, murder, and the like.

Perhaps we can grasp the importance of gathering information by looking at Rita's experience.

Rita's husband became involved in an affair with an emotionally disturbed woman. He eventually broke off the relationship and tried to repair the damage he'd done to Rita, whom he still loved. But Rita couldn't forgive her husband or the other woman. It was bad enough he'd had an affair—but to choose such a wretchedly unhappy and abused woman over her added insult to injury.

Inadvertently, Rita learned the history of the other woman. As a little girl, she'd often been made to bend naked over the bathtub while her father beat her with a belt until blood ran down her legs. As a friend told Rita this story, she found tears running down her cheeks. Any little girl raised by such a criminally abusive father might wind up seducing men in a desperate search for a man's love. The information also lent credibility to her husband's story that he'd first befriended the woman because he felt sorry for her . . . then felt affectionate toward this "hurting soul" . . . until the lines between affection and sexual involvement blurred. Further searching unearthed events in her husband's life that explained his vulnerability to such a strange relationship.

It didn't happen overnight, but the more Rita understood these facts, the more she was able to relinquish her
anger and pain. She could truly forgive, and sincerely pray
for the woman. Understanding was not condoning the
affair. And much work had to be done to heal her
husband's past to prevent further offenses.

But for Rita, the restoration process took a step forward
when the truth was known.

4. Allow information to become insight.

The longest distance in the world can be the distance
between the head and the heart. Once the facts are clear,
we might imagine that forgiveness would automatically
occur. Once again, our humanity gets in the way of
forgiving. Our self-protective and vengeful impulses can
pitch us into rounds of self-pity and bitter anger.

It takes heroic effort—real willpower—to move
beyond our own pain to understand what prevents us from
saying, "I forgive you."

In her book *The Hiding Place,* Corrie ten Boom
describes the most extreme abuses imaginable perpetrated
on her and the other inmates of a Nazi concentration camp
during World War II. Months after the war was over,
Corrie was traveling through Germany speaking in
churches about God's love and forgiveness. Inwardly,
though, she knew her words had a hollow sound.

After speaking in a church in Munich, she was
approached by a man she recognized as one of her former
guards, a particularly cruel one. He'd regained a semblance
of humanity, and smiled brightly as he talked about his
newfound faith in God. Looking Corrie in the eye, he held
out his hand. "Fraulein, if you can forgive me then I'll
know what you say is true, that God forgives me."

She was gripped by a terrible conflict. She wanted to

turn her back on this man—or do violence to him. In her mind's eye she could see her father and sister, who were both killed by the Nazis. She'd wanted to forgive what had happened to her . . . this moment brought insight as to why she'd been unable to do more than speak hollowly about forgiveness. She was daily reliving the horror of the camp.

In that moment, too, Corrie knew that she would continue to be haunted by old feelings and memories if she did not move beyond them. This was her chance . . . but could she do it?

Her arm remained frozen at her side, while the man's remained outstretched. As he gaped at her, Corrie prayed for strength she could not find in herself. And so she gave her will over to God, unable to change it on her own. Coldly, she stuck out her hand and clasped the palm of her former enemy.

"In that moment," she later wrote, "something miraculous happened. A current seemed to pass from me to him, while into my heart sprang a love for this stranger that almost overwhelmed me."

Forgiveness, as we've said, *is* a gift of God's grace. What Corrie described—the healing of one heart, the freeing of another—is a true miracle. The wonder of it is that God both gives us insight into our own heart *and* involves us with Him in the freeing of another.

5. Choose to relinquish the whole event.

It was, interestingly, in a psychiatry class that Grace says she learned relinquishment.

The class was discussing how to let go of past tragedies and trauma that hurt and scar. The professor asked the class to be silent for a moment and to watch him. One man, Lou, had been weeping copiously, obviously reliving some pain of his own.

"Lou," the professor ordered, "I want you to wrap up that handkerchief and hold it tightly in your hand." After a long silence, he said, "Now, let it fall." The bunched handkerchief landed on the floor. "How simple it was," says Grace. "But how very difficult to let go!"

In a few moments, Lou reached down to pick up his handkerchief. But another student observed him and suggested that this was the way we all tried to "pick up our old burdens again." With a smile now, Lou left the handkerchief there.

Grace says, "We all saw that it's our choice—an act of our will—that sets us free from burdens of the past."

IMPORTANT CHANGES WITHIN

When we forgive, significant changes take place within us.

Angie had some major forgiving to do after her husband had an affair. At one point in their tenuous relationship, Angie was separated from Jack and planning on a divorce. She felt hurt, angry, and put down, displaced by his cute young secretary.

Jack woke up to how wrong and foolish he'd been. He asked Angie to take him back. After much thought and prayer, she did.

Angie described the differences in her after she completed the forgiveness process we're describing.

First, the hurt was gone. She understood that it was not she who was undesirable, but her husband who felt needy and inadequate. Because Angie gave her pain to God, she felt bitterness being replaced by a new, more mature kind of love for Jack than she'd had before—God's love. She recognized she'd gained a level of understanding and compassion that could enable her to help other women in similar situations.

Second, a stronger, healthier Angie set clear boundaries before reconciling with Jack. She would not tolerate any impropriety with another woman again. As this new strength of character emerged, she found that she was mature enough not to resort to being "merely judgmental." She could speak the truth in love (Ephesians 4:15) and confront people's mistakes gently but honestly.

Third, she became a help to others in their struggles because she could help them see not only the faults of their offenders but their own weaknesses and need for maturing, as well. She could help them identify areas of weakness in which they needed to grow personally as they learned to forgive.

Finally, over time Angie's personal growth made her a wise, graceful, and compassionate wife and friend. She'd learned that life doesn't always follow the script we'd like it to. She came to see that life can actually be *better* than we imagined, if we press through wrongs done to us and help to create a healthy new future.

To this point, we've spoken about principles of forgiveness in a general sense. In the next two chapters, Grace will tell you how she learned the lessons of forgiveness during one of the most challenging times anyone could imagine.

CHAPTER FIVE

A PERSONAL RECKONING

BOTH DAVID AND I (GRACE SPEAKING) KNOW THAT IT'S NOT wise to use your own personal experience in an attempt to create universal principles to apply to other people. For that reason, we've relied on the authority of Jesus' teaching as the foundation for this book.

I have been a Christian since an early age and had heard many sermons about forgiveness. I now think, looking back, that I didn't know nearly enough about forgiveness—that is, the process of forgiveness we're describing in this book. I *thought* I understood forgiveness, and encouraged it in my counseling clients. Yes, I knew how to "let go" of smaller, and even some greater, offenses without seeking revenge or a payback of some kind. But I know now, after going through the most challenging passage of my life, that I was weak in my understanding of what it takes to walk it through when an offense takes place that seems impossible to forgive.

As I said, this book is founded on Jesus' teaching and not my own simple thoughts. And yet it was my personal experience— one of those terrible "crucible" times of life—that led to this book. And so I think it's only fair to step out from behind the counselor's desk now and, figuratively, sit beside you as a fellow traveler on the path of spiritual growth. It's time to tell you how I came to a point where I was sure I could *not* forgive the one person who shared all of life's intimacies with me—consequently, the one who had the power to hurt me most—my own husband.

I say that my husband, Herb Ketterman, was the one person who shared all of life's intimacies with me. That was true in a way. We lived together in Christian marriage for decades, raised fine children to adulthood together, and saw each other through the tough work it takes to build successful careers—he in business and medicine and I in medical and counseling practices.

Looking back, though, I know there were places inside Herb Ketterman I really could not go. Not that he was secretive. He was a wonderful, happy man who raised my spirits and was fun to be around. But there was also a certain limit, a door inside Herb I dimly sensed I couldn't open until and unless he chose to open it to me. Sometimes, even early in our marriage, I felt "left out" of his heart and a little sad—but not enough to make a huge issue of it.

If I think back to my rationalizations for not doing the work it takes to get inside Herb's head more, they seem pretty valid. For one thing, we were in the busiest years of our lives, raising kids, advancing our work. For another, I knew that marriage requires measures of acceptance and even tolerance. You don't make an issue of every petty thing, every time you feel hurt or left out.

And for another, I understood Herb's background and what made him the man I was attracted to—a quietly strong, hard-working man—a pillar I felt I could always lean on.

Two "Good" People Headed for Disaster

Herb was the third of four children born to a couple who were teachers. His father was a school principal in a series of small towns. Due to a hasty temper and some lack of diplomacy, he moved frequently from one school to another. During the years of the Great Depression, life was very difficult for this family. Herb's mother was an excellent teacher, but believed she should stay at home with their children until they were all in school. His father's angry temper resulted in some very harsh punishments, but there were many happy times as well. Herb still believes his father's punishments were deserved and does not think of them as abusive. What this disciplined atmosphere taught him was to work hard and toe the line at all times. If you are wrong, you deserve punishment and correction.

Little is known about his father's side of the family. But it was Herb's maternal grandfather who provided some security in their times of economic distress during the Depression—security and a model. He was a cattle rancher on the northern plains of Kansas and could tally years of riches, spoiled by occasional disasters. He was the storybook epitome of the crusty, golden-hearted rancher of his time. There were numerous uncles, aunts, and cousins connected to this patriarch. And from him, Herb learned why it was good for a man to work hard and never quit, even if exhaustion and the weather itself is against you: because other people need someone to depend on, and so many people depended on a man.

In this way, Herb came to admire his grandfather, and felt a drive to become as rich in material holdings as he was. He had the good business sense of his granddad and was open to risk.

Not that Herb was all business, or even the hard-hearted, shrewd business type. He had a compassionate side—in fact, he practiced family medicine for some thirty years—and a spiritual side, too. It was during his time in the armed forces that Herb was introduced to a personal faith in Jesus Christ. His family had been church-going, but for some reason personal faith was never discussed. After a good deal of study and questioning, Herb committed his life to Christ.

Serving God was a commitment and a challenge to Herb. He was a leader in the student Christian group he chose in college.

He was generous and self-sacrificing to many in need—a "real man of God"—which is one of the most powerful reasons I was drawn to him.

I was the sixth of seven children born to godly parents. They were products of uncounted generations of the "Plain People," stern Mennonites from Germany who settled for some 150 years in Lancaster County, Pennsylvania. While it was this commitment to God that brought Herb and me together, there were also big differences in other values we both inherited—which would work like invisible undercurrents in our marriage for years, setting us up for a disaster we could never foresee.

My mother's father became involved in the early Wesleyan Methodist movement. He was called to minister to pioneers and Native American people in Kansas. On one of his journeys home to raise funds for his ministry, he met my grandmother. She was converted to his beliefs and fell in love with him. All alone, and against the warnings of her loved ones, she boarded a train headed west. There her beloved Jacob took her hand as she stepped down to the wooden platform at Peabody, Kansas. They were married and settled there on the prairies they came to love. Together they served the Lord, thanking Him for the joys and enduring the heartaches He allowed—such was their view of Providence—including the births of three children who lived and two who were buried in the grassy plains.

From this tradition, I received the blessing of knowing that our lives and our circumstances rest in God's hands. We can trust God, and go about our small business while He works out the things greater than we can handle.

Despite the tight bonds of their Mennonite tradition, my father and one of his sisters shifted their faith to that of my mother, Wesleyan Methodist. Adding the fervor of that group to the ancient fundamentals of his past made a staunch theology that pervaded my early years. Family prayers were daily. We went to church twice on Sundays, and once more during each week.

We also attended regular and lengthy "camp meetings" and revival services. Laughter and games were a big part of our lives. Yet I came to understand that rules were many and must be strictly kept.

My early life, I confess, was simple and straightforward. Whereas Herb's life held some uncertainty—what with his father's frequent job changes and moves—mine was filled with certainty. I remember love, the exuberance of joy-filled experiences, and the excitement of discoveries, curiosity, and adventure. The simple certainty of my life can be summed up, in a way, by one of my best memories.

When I was a little girl, Dad loved to have me ride at his side on various farm vehicles we owned. When he'd pull up, out in a field or at the barn, he'd jump down first. Then he'd turn back and, with his big, rough hands outstretched to me, say, "Now jump, Gracie!"

Gleefully, I leapt into those arms made strong by farm work. As he held me for an instant, I could look into his twinkling brown eyes, and just before he set me down I snuggled against his chest. Then I would skip happily along beside this man who I knew would never let me fall.

How simple it was, when I committed my life to God at nine, to transfer the same kind of utter trust to a heavenly Father. Knowing I was His child provided the security for eternity that Dad had given me for my youth.

Dad was my earliest, strongest supporter—but not my only one by any means. Later, as a young woman, I scored fairly high on I.Q. tests. My heaven-sent pastor was absolutely thrilled and became my best advocate, encouraging me to apply for medical school because the healing professions interested me.

Without his boost, my aims would have been a good bit lower. His support, plus my father and mother's prayers and steep sacrifices, got me into pre-med at the University of Kansas.

After two years in a small, cloistered denominational college,

I faced the nearly overwhelming adjustment to a large state university campus—which was teeming with newly discharged war veterans.

For the first time, my simple sense of security was shaken.

I was feeling overwhelmed and lonely. In order to help me through this, a compassionate physics professor introduced me to a solid Christian group on campus. The simple faith of my girlhood was enriched by the discipling that came from in-depth Bible studies and sound teaching I received from this ministry. This was just what I needed to help answer my questions raised by the godless humanism I was encountering for the first time in several of my courses.

At the same time, I needed something on the human level, too. I was a normal (if somewhat sheltered) young woman who was sensing the need for someone to count on—someone I could depend on to be a steadying pillar as I faced this vast, unfolding, challenging, real world that was opening before me.

It was in this physical and emotional setting that my road and Herb Ketterman's crossed.

Socially, Herb was light years ahead of my bumbling, country girl ways. One evening, after Bible study, he patted the arm of his chair, inviting me to sit beside him. "C'mon, Gracie. Sit down and tell me all about it."

Shyly, I responded, "All about what?"

"Oh," he answered, "just anything you like!"

In a way, it was like an invitation to jump from the precarious and uncertain atmosphere of college into the solid and open arms of someone who was just *for me*. From the first, this farm girl with dreams of "caring for people" fell for the quiet but definite drive of this caring young man with a steel resolve who seemed destined to be a pillar in the medical and business community, and in the Christian community as well.

Neither of us could have known what we were in for.

DREAMS UNWIND

Herb and I fell in love. We married when Herb was certain of his admission into medical school. He'd served in the army, and so we were able to live—frugally—on Herb's veteran's check and some odd jobs we had time for. When I had med school exams, Herb would iron my white intern's uniforms. When he needed help, I gladly did what I could. Besides the practical help, we both understood what the other was going through—at least in terms of schooling. From the first, much of our marriage was based on a healthy interdependence.

If you are years into your marriage, you'll understand how quickly the years, even decades, seem to pass. Life picks up a pace, and the years begin to roll.

Internships were followed by new practices. Our first child, a daughter, was followed by a son, then another daughter, each one enriching our lives immeasurably. Our lives were filled with church activities, work with the Christian Medical Society, and volunteering in our community.

Through these unfolding years, I saw Herb becoming the man I'd dreamed he could be. He was a caring father who worried that his demanding career was keeping him from being everything he wanted to be as a dad. Still, he was there for our children as much as he could be, through grade school, then high school, and as college loomed ahead. Along with this busy family life, Herb was also an excellent Sunday school teacher, a gifted member of several boards, a man faithful and generous in giving.

Yet I must admit that there was a side to Herb that always seemed under pressure. At times, when pressures within and without made him testy—often, with me—I didn't know what to do. It was not in me to confront and stand up for myself. My usual response involved letting my feelings be crushed, withdrawing from him a bit emotionally, then rationalizing away

Herb's shortness: He *was* under pressure after all, and he was a good father, a caring man who carried the load of his patients' well-being with him. Who wouldn't get testy?

One issue that gave me misgivings was Herb's drive to become wealthy. I'd known this was one of his dreams from our early days. I thought it would be nice, certainly, but I didn't share this dream with anything like the same intensity. One day, years into our marriage, Herb shared with me that he believed we could become really rich—millionaires, perhaps. Something in this dream made me uncomfortable. Maybe it seemed to me that it was becoming more a compulsion than a life goal, but I couldn't say that for certain. To be honest, I recall a small uneasiness, like a foreboding, a sense that the ambition to become rich had been the undoing of more than one man.

And to be honest in another way, the pressures of our life had crept up on us and taken a toll at that point. Herb's testiness had become more habitual and, over the years, it had been easier and easier for him to let it out at me if I objected, raised a contrary opinion, or resisted his plans in some way. Early in our marriage I'd felt he was a man in whose arms I could relax and be my honest, simple farm-girl self; now I felt like I got my proverbial hand slapped any time I truly disagreed.

The strange thing is, I'd moved on in my career—from a medical practice in pediatrics to a psychiatric counseling practice based in Christian principles—and though I thought of myself as a forthright person committed to honesty as a good rule of both health and spirituality, in relation to Herb I truly was not honest. I developed a way of operating with him that skirted honesty. Sure, I might hint at, or state, a misgiving or disagreement one time. But if the whiff of conflict came my way—if Herb's eyes got dark and intense, or he drummed his fingers, or his voice grew louder and his manner insistent—I retreated from the conflict. But in retreating, I carried a wound. Why couldn't my husband respect, honor, and just *listen* to me? Why didn't I feel "safe" enough with him to risk conflict? After all, he'd never even raised a hand to me.

So a pattern developed and, like rain running down one of those Kansas farm roads of my girlhood, in time it created a rut in our relationship . . . and in more time, a virtual chasm. Herb pushed; I retreated feeling hurt; then I rationalized. In the case of Herb's ambition to be rich, I knew many organizations that would be able to help so many more needy people if they had the funds, and we could help supply those funds if we had more money.

Despite my rationalizing, though, I knew something was deeply wrong between us. I was old enough, and experienced enough with counseling, to know that life and marriage are not all the dreams our idealizing youth hoped for. But what was wrong between us felt worse than a little bit of dashed dreams. It felt like estrangement—and, seeing what I saw in counseling couples when dreams unwound so far they could not be put together again, a small sense of dread and unhappiness took hold.

OUR MARRIAGE UNRAVELS

It was about this time, several decades into our marriage, that Herb began what he later called a "spiritual drift." His time and energy had to be carefully divided among his work, his hobbies, his investments, his family, and our church. Every one of these areas pulled at him for attention—and not only did each priority begin to suffer, he began to suffer.

As Herb felt his energies and his spirit straining to the limits, he also began to think he might never achieve his ambition to be, like his granddad, successful in achieving great wealth. During this time, a real estate agent who was a member of our church solicited Herb to be his business partner in an exciting plan. They would invest in land that was undervalued now but was slated to be developed into high-priced residential neighborhoods and a couple of business districts. It was the potential "gold mine" he'd been hoping for. Joining as a partner with this man, Herb bought into the plan, which began with buying or building four motels. At first, it seemed they were on their way, as local businesses promised to keep the motels profitably full.

Herb had developed a motto: "Opportunity is often the best bargain!" I'd come to dislike that phrase. The cost of this "golden opportunity" seemed no bargain to me. Expenses, and risks, were great. Fear and misgiving made me overcome my retreating side, and I pleaded with Herb to slow down his expenditures.

Instead, he moved full-steam ahead.

My fears only grew when the investments did not become greatly profitable as quickly as we had hoped. To support the investments, Herb was forced to increase his medical practice. He loved his work and the families he served so benevolently. But now he felt pressured, and was often gone from home for eighty or more hours a week. Being a physician myself—and a rationalizer—I knew one could not deny medical care to patients, no matter how many there were. Still, I felt powerless to find a way to help Herb slow down—powerless to get him to come home to us.

Now Herb regularly missed church, and rarely had time for the morning devotions the kids and I shared over breakfast.

I must admit, Herb tried heroically to stay involved with our children. Somehow he managed to find time for their school and sports events. But in order to help him in this, I increasingly gave up my time with him, which added to the chasm between us, not to mention my growing sense of resentment and self-pity. I began to nag. I withdrew support. Frankly, I had no more to give, and didn't know what else to do. Overtaxed and overwhelmed, Herb couldn't see he was nearing the end of his resources.

For some time we lived in an increasingly distant, empty marriage. All it would take was one quake, and the chasm between us would split wide open.

That quake came in the early 1980s, when the national economy went through upheaval. Interest rates shot from 6 percent to over 20 percent. Banks that had been eager to loan money to Herb suddenly demanded the payoff. Herb's partner, so eager to involve him in investments, offered no help. In desperation, Herb even resorted to selling a treasured coin collection to help pay his debts. Due to the recession, it brought less than its appraised value, hardly enough to dent the debts he owed. All he could think to do was work harder and harder to take care of his responsibilities and live up to his old picture of himself—a man others could totally depend on.

Then came several personal blows. Herb's mother, with whom he'd been very close, died, adding grief to his load. Then, tragically, his nurse suffered a heart attack in the office. Despite Herb's best efforts, he could not save her. She died in the ambulance en route to the hospital. Next, one of the two women who kept his business affairs in order moved away. To top it off, our youngest child—the last at home—had gone away to college.

By now, comforting Herb was impossible. Trying to get his attention didn't work. I could no longer reach the man who'd been such an intimate part of me. My own loss and grief felt inconsolable. Over and over, I rehearsed my losses:

I lost my ideal spouse. The man who'd been with me during the rigors of medical school, the births of our children, the establishment of my pediatric practice, and my subsequent choice of more training in order to practice psychiatry—*this* man was gone. I judged him to be a self-serving man who had no time for me.

I lost my dreams. Early on, we'd dreamed of someday doing medical missions work. Herb no longer held that dream.

I lost my companion. Weekend trips that once served as brief "honeymoons" were no more. When we were out together, Herb's attention focused more on our companions than on me.

I lost my financial security. The good standard of living we'd enjoyed had been swallowed up in the service of Herb's ambition to become a millionaire. Ahead lay mountains of debt.

Worst of all, *I lost hope.* All of my efforts to stop Herb's drift, to recapture our relationship, to resurrect the man I'd fallen in love with, failed.

Something else was wrong, too, but I would not let myself look at it. It was hard enough to face one awful truth: Our marriage was in ruins.

Breaking the Bonds

Herb and I passed each other in the halls of the home we'd built together—passed each other with coldness, sometimes hostility. There were intense arguments, followed by numbness.

After the most concentrated period of prayer and searching, I decided that if I had any love left, it had to be "tough love." I challenged Herb to accept counseling with me; if he refused, I'd seek a separation. A few sessions with an excellent therapist ended when the man felt Herb was unwilling to deal with the real issues. Herb seemed just as happy not to go.

When that effort failed, I felt I was left with no other healthy choice.

Never will I forget the cold January morning when I found myself walking, against my will, into the office of an attorney. Some time later I walked out, having filed for a divorce from the man with whom I'd shared my life for over thirty-five years. He could, of course, change the picture by making an honest effort to change. But the very fact that I'd filed for divorce was, as people say, "unreal."

You must know, I didn't take this step lightly. I'd always written and lectured against divorce. I believed that intelligent adults could work through their differences, negotiate, and reestablish harmony. I had counseled many couples along that very path. Yet I could not accomplish these things. I'd believed that "love would win"—yet my love hadn't reached Herb's heart. Before I'd made my decision, you can believe I sought counsel and solicited prayers for God's guidance. And at last I knew what I had to do.

In hindsight, I think I was learning lessons about "tough love"—it just wasn't one that's in the book of "Christian lessons." I'm not recommending that everyone who feels trapped in a failed marriage should run out and file for divorce. Even as a counselor who was used to giving tough advice, filing for divorce made me feel devastated, like a failure, frightened, angry, and confused.

Even so—though some will not accept this statement—I clung to a sense that I was following God's guidance. I needed to follow God in a path of obedience that forced me to leave behind my rescuing and enabling kind of "love." For me, a drastic parting was necessary—a path so extremely hard that I'd not wish it on anyone else.

These were hard steps, as I said, and I couldn't find the courage to tell Herb I'd filed for divorce. Fortunately, a mutual friend helped me out and told Herb she'd learned of my decision. Another friend, recently separated from his wife, offered to let him move in temporarily. In the end, I wrote a letter and, as kindly as possible, explained my repeated pain caused by his neglect and rejection.

He was stunned—then hurt, then sad, then angry.

Once I'd made the decision, oddly, I could face fears I'd held a long time. Intuitively, I *knew* there was another woman in Herb's life. He was just "gone" on too many occasions, and there were many times his answering service couldn't find him. Long gone was his interest in our once exciting romantic getaways, and he was indifferent to my attempts at affection. On one occasion, I'd come home in the wee hours of the morning to find him gone. He was nowhere to be found. When I questioned him the next day, he became angry. Guilt was written all over his face. And then there were all the hang-up phone calls.

Now, with Herb out of the house—soon to be out of my life—my hurt turned to anger. Nothing I'd done could penetrate the thick wall Herb had built against me. What had I done to deserve this? What insanity was this—to think he could do as he pleased and expect me to *accept* it?

After filing for divorce, Herb did make an effort. We wept together. He assured me he loved me and could change—words I'd heard before, words I wanted to believe. I knew I had to find courage to hold my ground, and I said, "This time you'll have to *show* me you've changed."

For months, Herb kept insisting I should relent and that he'd changed. Then abruptly, in frustration, he turned on me one day: "Most women would be glad to have a husband like me."

In Herb's eyes, *I* was at fault. My "tough love" approach had failed. Strangely, I felt at peace as I prayed, *Okay, Lord—now what?*

After that confrontation, I knew there was only one thing to do: finalize the divorce, and in so doing acknowledge the truth—that there was no longer anything to hold us together.

The bonds of our marriage were broken. Only God knew why—but so far He wasn't shedding any light on it for me.

In a year, the divorce was final.

TRUTH COMES TO LIGHT

I could hear the house phone ringing as I pulled into the garage one evening. It had been a full day with an early staff meeting. Inside, I was tempted to let the ringing go on until the caller gave up. But in the end, I picked up.

Herb was on the other end. "I'm in jail, Grace. I've been arrested. Don't hang up on me—I need you."

Now the truth I'd been waiting for began to unfold.

My fears that Herb was involved with another woman were facts he now confirmed. He told me he'd become involved with a woman who, along with her teenaged daughter, was trapped in bad financial circumstances. Their poverty and need got his attention, and his first efforts to help them were "only financial"— but then came a moment's vulnerability . . . a lapse . . . and he'd become sexually involved.

As he spoke I kept thinking, *I knew he was having an affair.* But I wasn't ready for the stunner.

Yes, he'd been a fool to let the stress of his financial situation allow him to seek escape in the arms of these women. What a complete idiot not to see this woman was using her daughter as bait. . . .

I was numb as his words sank in. Herb had not only been with a woman, but had also been inappropriately affectionate with her daughter . . . her *teenaged* daughter.

When Herb tried to break it off with the woman and get himself out of the situation, her anger and betrayal were inevitable. She notified the authorities that Herb had been involved with a minor, exaggerating his behavior. Detectives had surprised Herb at his office only hours before, handcuffed him, and took him to jail.

Even in my shock, I could not imagine the utter humiliation Herb had to be suffering. To many he'd been a pillar in the church, in the community—and there were our children to think of. He was disgraced. Reduced to a jail cell, and to one pleading phone call.

Despite the mix of pain and anger that was now flooding me, I also felt a countering wave. In Herb's voice, I heard the sound of a truly broken soul. And at that, I believe I experienced a miracle of God's grace. In words not my own, I found myself trying to console Herb—knowing his pride, I sensed he could try to take his own life.

"Hold steady," I told him. *"Don't hurt yourself.* The children and I will stand by you. This crisis can be the turning point we've needed."

At this exact moment, Herb's time was up. The phone cut off.

As I made more calls, to a lawyer, to friends, I realized something in my heart was trying to change. I'd given God free space to work in Herb's life, to bring hidden issues to light—to break the pride that had driven him to seek success at all costs. I'd never bargained for this.

Another question was about to present itself: Was I willing to let God continue to work in *my* life?

Making a Choice

Our private tragedy became citywide titillating news. On TV and radio, in the newspaper and even in national magazines, an exaggerated version of Herb's story appeared. We learned how quickly people believe the worst.

Still, we were blessed with dear friends who heard the sordid details and yet stood by us. Several spent the evening of the "fateful phone call" with me. They loved me and affirmed their love for Herb. They helped me to post bond and release Herb from jail.

Our dear friend and retired pastor listened to me struggling for words to explain my mix of feelings. "You understand Herb now, don't you?" he said. I nodded. "You want to forgive him, too, don't you?" Another nod.

"Grace," he challenged, "if you really mean what you say, you need to go and visit Herb in the morning."

Now it was one thing to mouth words of forgiveness. It would be quite another to put action with those words.

In the morning, this same man drove me downtown. After some tracking, I learned Herb had been taken to his arraignment. No one knew which, of a hundred possible hearing rooms, he was in. *What am I doing here?* I thought. *I'm divorced from this man. Just walk away.* Standing in the noisy hallway, with strangers and clerks jostling me—with terrible pain in my head and my heart—I came to the moment of reckoning.

I could choose between a way I knew to be spiritually, emotionally, and mentally healthy—or choose what my aching head and tired body were telling me to do. I didn't create this mess, and I didn't want to go back to being the enabler I'd always been.

Even as I argued with myself, I knew this was different: Herb was not in the hands of a wife who could never press him and make him accountable, he was in the hands of civil authorities who were dead-set to prosecute. And there had been the shamed, remorseful tone. . . .

I could feel the pulse in my throbbing temple the moment I chose, without any emotion at all, to be at his side whatever this cost him. If I had to look in every hearing room in this huge building, I would find him . . . and I'd forgive him, whatever that cost me.

I took it as a sign that God was in this mess with us when I found Herb in the very first room I checked. I also found the courage to walk into that room full of curious people, to sit directly behind Herb, and touch him on the back. He looked terrible after a sleepless night and, knowing how awful his mouth would feel, I offered him a stick of gum.

After the hearing, the judge, whom I knew well from my work with prisoners, kindly allowed me to speak with Herb before the guards hauled him away. This man who had been the "boss" so long was indeed as helpless and contrite in spirit as I'd guessed. When I told him I forgave him, his eyes glistened.

We were, that day, launched on a five-year journey in which we had no choice but to walk through the fire of our circumstances — circumstances I believe God allowed to bring the truth to light. For it's only by bringing dark things into the light that reconciliation is possible.

WALKING THROUGH THE FIRE

Herb's court session was a nightmare. Because he was a prominent doctor, TV cameras and news reporters thronged the sidewalk outside the court. We were the subject of ribald jokes, catcalls, even threats.

By this time, our family had suffered greatly from the impact of the publicity and scandal. Many in Herb's profession had ostracized him, as did some Christians. He could not resume his practice, and the financial struggles grew even worse. Herb became deeply depressed, emotionally exhausted, and suicidal. We convinced him a hospital stay was necessary. There he experienced more healing through the loving forgiveness of our three children, as each one reassured Dad of his worth and dearness to them.

Slowly, painfully, we walked through the fire. Most of our church family stood lovingly by us.

Regularly, I asked God to show me what lessons I needed to learn. Some had condemned me for divorcing. Yet I knew I'd had to, as the expression of tough love. As I continued to pray and seek counsel, I got the message: The lessons in *this* end of the fire were mainly for Herb. God was, in His own way, chastising a son whom He loved.

In a closed session with only a judge, the prosecutor, and Herb's lawyer present, he pleaded guilty. He did so both to own up and to avoid a jury trial. Ironically, if he'd opted for a longer trial by jury, the truth might have come out. Only at the sentencing did we realize what a mistake pleading guilty had been. The sentence: *five to twenty years in prison.* A devastating blow.

The prison journey was an arduous one, too detailed to go into here. I'll only tell you I traveled one hour each way, every weekend, to visit Herb under the worst possible circumstances. Finally, face to face, Herb and I had nothing else to do but talk. And talk we did.

Visiting was no joy. Sitting in unbearable heat, I often listened as Herb railed and talked out his bitterness. Where was the tone of humility I'd heard? Now it seemed ironic that Herb was so bitter, when *I* was the one who—having been betrayed, rejected, verbally abused—had the "right" to be bitter. During one visit I told him, "I understand your anger and bitterness. You've lost a lot. And anger is part of grieving over a loss. But I've lost a lot, too. Here's what I propose. I'll listen to your anger for *fifteen minutes per visit.* Then let's talk about better things. If you don't respect this, I'll quit visiting."

He did respect my boundary on this, and as the weeks slowly ticked by his bitterness gradually lessened. As he began to *really* listen to me, I explained why I'd filed for divorce. I was also able to see that in disagreements, I'd usually believed I was right, automatically making him wrong—and was surprised to see that he'd come to view me as self-righteous. But then, we don't see ourselves as others see us, do we?

To be sure, my mistakes were no excuses for Herb's. But a wise psychiatrist friend taught me that when you give up having to be right, it creates a climate more conducive to the other giving up being wrong. Facing the truth about myself helped stop our power struggle. Besides, it was the only honest thing to do.

Finally, I'll never forget the day when he said, "You know, Gracie, being in prison may have saved my life. I was living with so much stress; I don't see how I could have survived it much longer."

To me, this was *the* major turning point. Herb was able to recognize a bit of God's tough love.

Slowly, over months and years, our love came back to life. It grew to be even more beautiful than before—not as romantic, but more mature and realistic.

We know now that few loves have had to go through the maelstrom of fire ours did. And we both realize now what a miracle it is. It was another miracle when Herb was released from prison after only four years and two months.

And it was not the last miracle.

BEGINNING AGAIN

After Herb was released from prison, we waited two years. And, yes, we decided to remarry.

Our second marriage, you can well imagine, is *very* different from, and far better, than our first. Our communication is open. I have stopped nagging (mostly), and Herb is willing to recognize and express needs and feelings (sometimes!).

Both of us know we've come through the fire with a strength and wisdom we couldn't have gained any other way.

I've told you our story at some length because I want you to understand I am not doling out glib or "nice" Christian advice when I speak about the need to forgive. I want you to know that

I know forgiveness is costly. Here are some of the costs to me:

My pride. Because I forgave Herb, I chose to face the public humiliation of going to the courtroom before a judge with whom I'd worked. I knew he'd pity me, and my pride was shot. This was just the beginning. But I found a dignity and peace that comes only from doing what one knows is right.

Expending energy to cope with Herb's initial bitterness and blame. I wanted to rail at him, but instead had to listen to him railing at me, until I set firm boundaries for him.

Expending time and energy to encourage Herb. It was not a pleasure to drive for an hour twice every weekend, in heat or snow. But seeing our relationship being resurrected was a valid reward. Ongoing work with other inmates and their families continues to cost—yet I know we help them.

Bearing blame and rejection. Two groups refused to allow me to keep seminar appointments I had previously arranged. They were Christian groups, and I had to struggle to forgive their lack of forgiveness. Not a single secular group treated me in that way. It was amazing to see God give me an authenticity beyond any past experience.

Bearing ridicule and condemnation. A physician acquaintance told me that most doctors judged me to be "the most codependent person in the city." Because I had functioned very productively, alone, for over five years, I was able to ignore that. But I didn't miss the irony: I was condemned by some for divorcing Herb and by others for standing by him.

Watching my reputation suffer. I had to give up caring about what others thought of me—though this was a happy price. Because I was getting flak from both ends, I could clearly see that this was not a popularity contest I could ever hope to win. I learned to say with the apostle Paul, "But with me it is a very small thing that I should be judged of you, or of man's judgment; yea, I judge not mine own self . . . but He that judgeth me is the Lord" (1 Corinthians 4:3,4, KJV).

Sharing in the pain this event inflicted on others. Our children were horribly grieved by their father's wrongdoing. Herb's siblings and mine were also embarrassed and traumatized by this event. A brother who lived in our town discussed moving away. My daughter-in-law tried to avoid using her surname because "Ketterman" is not as common as "Smith." My oldest daughter, studying for her Ph.D. in psychology, was horrified to hear her father being used as a bad example in her university class. It cost me a massive amount of energy to reassure each of these people dear to me and to maintain my own identity.

For These Costs

For these costs, however, I must tell you that I acquired a whole new awareness: *I have learned who I am in Christ,* and that knowledge is priceless! I now know that indeed I *can* do all things through Christ who strengthens me!

The cost of forgiving has bought, for both Herb and me, the gems of redemption and reconciliation.

And these spiritual gems, to me, are priceless.

CHAPTER SIX

STRENGTH FOR THE LONG HAUL

W HEN I (GRACE AGAIN) SEE PICTURES OF MYSELF AS A GIRL, or as a young bride, I shake my head. Never could I have imagined the events just narrated in the previous chapter.

In over thirty-five years of practice as a physician, it was my privilege to help others through crises. I'd listened to and cared about others' heartaches. But our crisis was like a raging forest fire burning out of control, and its devastation lingered long.

In fact, its real effects are with us to this day, especially where finances are concerned. At this phase of our lives, when we could be restfully enjoying the fruit of our labors, this is not to be.

I tell you this because the truth about forgiveness is that it is both a matter of choosing at one point in time which impulse you will follow *and* it is also a path you must follow every day thereafter as you continue to create the climate of attitudes that makes your forgiveness an ongoing reality. That's because, while we can choose to forgive even a life-shattering event, we have these marvelous brains that do not forget very easily.

Many of us are tricked by our memories into doubling back on our decisions. Something triggers the intensity of our past loss and our pain, like the anniversary of a child's death because of a drunk driver. Or the offender slips up and harms us again, in the same way or in another way. Immediately, the accusing and self-condemning voice comes back. *See, he hasn't changed at all. You were foolish to let him off the hook so easily.*

We become discouraged with the path Jesus offered us. We say to ourselves, *This is impractical, and it doesn't work,* or, *I just can't do it. I'm not a supersaint,* or, *I'm not cut out for this forgiveness stuff.*

The truth is, we must continue to build on the foundation of our first major choice to forgive until we have created inside ourselves the habit or spirit of forgiveness.

I have no doubt Jesus understood this need to form a new habit of spirit when He was asked the question, "How many times shall I forgive my brother when he sins against me? Up to seven times?" (Matthew 18:21). You can tell how greatly this disciple was infected by the pharisaical legalistic spirit, which always thinks in terms of "how much" and "how many." This spirit remains in us as long as we mete out forgiveness in careful measures, while part of us waits in the wings to see if forgiveness will "work"—and if it doesn't, we're ready to lavish on the punishment.

Jesus responded to this question, which came out of a petty, measuring mindset, this way: "I tell you, not seven times, but seventy times seven" (18:22).

I don't believe Jesus was just giving us a more generous number to shoot for and then we're done. He wasn't talking about counting and measuring at all. I believe Jesus was saying this: To successfully forgive—to replace the impulse to revenge—you must keep forgiving until it replaces hurt and anger. Even if that means you have to forgive the same life-shattering offense over and over every single time memory brings it up, and every time the accusing voice inside goads you to go back to your old way of reacting.

In an earlier chapter, we saw that the goal of forgiveness as it relates to the offended party is to keep one free from inner reactions that impair and ruin one's life long after the offense. As it relates to offenders, the goal of forgiveness is to give them time to consider their harmful actions and choose a new course that doesn't wound. What period of time? According to Jesus, the Master of forgiveness, reconciliation, and restoration—as long as it takes.

And so I want to continue my story and Herb's to show you what forgiveness means when you are in it for the long haul.

EFFORT

As I mentioned, the crisis I've described occurred in the mid-1980s. Some think I'm a fool to have remarried Herb; others marvel. But the real truth is, we are both learning more every day about the ongoing miracle of forgiveness. Because just as my forgiveness offers Herb a graceful space to examine his errors, his forgiveness offers me the same thing.

Today, Herb and I are better, and quicker, at forgiving. But with all the challenges that still lie before us—the little daily ones, and the major ones like our ongoing financial situation— forgiveness still requires effort.

I told you I was able to forgive Herb, somewhere between my phone conversation and my choice to find his hearing room, but I am no saint. Though I grew up in a "godly" family, as I told you, my family also lived by a clear, if unspoken, understanding: If you hurt me or anyone in this family, you are crossed off the list of friends forever. We would be courteous to you because that's the "Christian" thing to do, but never again would you be allowed to get close. Perhaps this is a bit exaggerated, but not much.

With this mindset built into the very foundation of my being, you can well imagine that—after my first, foundational struggle to forgive—it has taken ongoing effort to build on that foundation a well-formed habit of forgiveness.

What helps in the effort is another foundation stone. I must be candid. That foundation is simple faith. In choosing to forgive,

I also had to choose to believe that God, my heavenly Father, knows what's best for us. I had to trust that when He instructed us to forgive—and to do so until we can do it freely—the Creator of body and soul was telling us the best way to live. I'm sure He also knew it would be a costly process.

NEGOTIATING

The first cost to me has been to my self-image. I always saw myself as a forgiving person, but in fact I shifted between ineffective nagging and internalizing, or "stuffing," my hurt and anger. As I told you, I had to learn the new way of relating that must accompany forgiveness—that is, the way of establishing firm boundaries and negotiating the relationship.

It meant learning to say, as I said to Herb during the early prison visits, "This is what I need, and why I need you to do this. The relationship goes no further until and unless you can help me by meeting these terms." Herb, for his part, can do the same with me when it comes to his wants and needs. If it's not possible to meet each other's terms, we've had to learn to talk and *negotiate* until we agree on other acceptable terms.

Negotiation is a skill that helps the process of learning to forgive, let go, and move on. It's a life skill we can all benefit by learning.

Let's say you have a fairly simple, but chronic, issue between you and another person. One party may say, "I need to talk about [an important issue or a hurt]. I'd like to talk right now. Are you free to do this?" This makes the need known, and lets the other party know enough about the topic to prepare mentally and emotionally, if necessary. Notice that it's a request, not a demand. The other partner can respond by saying, "Okay, let's talk now," or can negotiate, saying, "I know this is important to you. But I [have a blistering headache, have a deadline with something I'm working on, am under pressure to help one of the kids]. Can we pick a time a little later to handle this?"

Louis immediately objected when the process of learning to negotiate was described to him. "Cara jumps all over me when she has a beef. She doesn't give me an inch, or take a half-second to consider that I might not be in the wrong." In this case, that "inch" of understanding, that "half-second" of thoughtfulness, *is* what Louis needs to negotiate.

"And at the same time," he goes on, "Cara stonewalls my attempts to talk about things that are bothering me. She says, 'The kids are hanging all over me, and I have a stack of reading to do for work.'" That is indeed "stonewalling" because Cara is blocking Louis's request and offering him no option. No wonder he feels unimportant and frustrated. A pattern of noncommunication like this cuts the bonds of affection and *must* be reversed.

Louis can both forgive Cara—which means not holding it against her even if, due to pressures she feels, she has to stall his requests most of the time—*and* he can also hold her firmly accountable in negotiating for her attention by saying, "Then you set the time when you can talk." He can even say, "But it's got to be in the next twenty-four hours."

Louis wonders, "What if she makes an excuse, or says, 'I know what's bothering you, and I don't want to talk about it again'?"

He can help the negotiation by saying, "Talking will benefit both of us. I don't want to attack and hurt you, I want to resolve some friction that's harming our marriage." He may also need to set a firm boundary: "I'm willing to wait until later, or tomorrow—but this *has* to be the very next thing we talk about. It's too important to ignore."

Negotiating is important in life's more difficult issues, too.

Jerry made a stop on the way home from work, when he'd promised Leslie he'd be home to meet their seven-year-old daughter, Jessica, as she stepped off the bus. On that September afternoon, as Jessica darted out from in front of the bus, a teenaged driver—ignoring the flashing lights—sped by and hit her. She was killed on impact.

Every September, as the anniversary of Jessica's death approached, Leslie went into deep depression. For weeks, she treated Jerry to a list of "if onlys." In guilty, mortified, silent pain, Jerry had to hear, "If only you'd been here. . . . " For many years he took this treatment, apologizing over and over, but believing Leslie's pain and accusation were his "just punishment."

Finally, the guilty pain triggered a downward spiral into alcoholism. Recognizing that this was a pit with no bottom, Jerry dragged himself to a counselor. Among other things, the counselor encouraged Jerry to negotiate with Leslie. Jerry had never considered that something as major as a mother's grief for her dead child can be helped by establishing healthy boundaries around it—and certainly never considered that he, "the guilty party," could help establish them.

With the counselor's coaching, Jerry asked Leslie to set aside a day to talk well in advance of the next anniversary, when her feelings were less likely to be intensified. He told her he needed to talk about Jessica's death.

That day, Jerry reminded Leslie of the many times he'd said he was sorry. He talked, actually for the first time, about the plaguing memories, the grief that he would never walk his little girl down the aisle at her wedding, the anguish he was trying to medicate with alcohol.

As he spoke, Jerry began to sob. "You have no idea how many times I've wished I was dead. How often I've wanted to blow my brains out. If I don't quit punishing myself, I know I'll drink myself to death. Somehow I can't believe that's right. But I can't take hearing you *blame* me over and over when you say, 'If only you'd been there. . . . '"

Facing Leslie, he insisted, "I miss my baby girl more than you'll ever know, Leslie. But can't we do something besides reliving that day every single year? Can you find another way to handle your grief? You go into depression every year. *And the whole thing is killing me.*"

Tears were streaming down Leslie's face now. "I—I had no idea what I was doing to you when I said that. I was angry at you, and hated you, at first. But I never really believed it was your fault. Can you forgive me for torturing you by saying those things?"

Jerry's courage in negotiating a boundary around Leslie's grief expressions was one of the healthiest things he could have done for either of them. Together, they decided to plant a flowering tree in the yard as a memorial. And Leslie's springtime expressions of wonder—"What a beautiful tree"—replaced her focus on the autumn grief. So Jerry's courage not only brought a moment of profound forgiveness, it also set in motion a process of healing that eased their grief and started to re-knit them together as a couple.

I mentioned that when Herb was in prison, we had nothing else to do but talk. Much of our talking was renegotiating. After thirty-five years of marriage *and* a divorce, you can believe there was a lot to renegotiate in terms of the different ways we approached *everything*—our feelings, our money, our dealings with each other and with our children, our careers, even our approach to faith. I can't think of anything that did not require some adjustment.

As I said in the last chapter, I'd never seen how insisting—*believing*—my way was right actually gave me an air of self-righteousness that had pushed Herb away from me. That characteristic was nowhere in my image of myself. Negotiating showed me otherwise, even as it helped us forgive.

LEARNING TO BEAR UP

Just as we need to resolve the conflicts we can resolve, learning to forgive over the long haul requires us to face and accept the things that cannot be changed.

For Leslie and Jerry, that meant accepting the loss of their daughter as an unchangeable reality. Once Jerry broke through the memories that played over in Leslie's mind by helping her to face *present realities,* she was able to face the fact that Jessica's death was "a thing of the past."

"It was like he broke a spell, or woke me from a hypnotic trance," Leslie admits. In fact, powerful memories *do* have something like a hypnotic effect on us, dropping a film of past reality down over present reality, and so we see *today* through the overlay of *yesterday.*

When we refuse to forgive, we constantly project old memories before our own eyes, and leave ourselves stuck in past realities, when we are meant to move on and heal. This doesn't negate the fact that *the damaging event of the past has also changed our present reality in ways that cannot be undone.*

In order to continue in an attitude of forgiving, it's necessary to grow in another mature skill—that is, *learning to bear our losses in a mature fashion.*

Frankly, many of us never want to grow up when it comes to bearing losses. Children cry, whine, blame, manipulate, get angry and throw tantrums, and insist or bully whenever the thing they're denied is even mentioned. To mature means that we accept several truths:

First, *the people in our lives are not perfect.* They are, in fact, riddled with flaws that will cause us harm as we live together.

Second, *loss and pain are a part of life—not only at the hands of strangers and circumstances, but even at the hands of people close to us.*

If we want to mature, we have to tear away the illusion we keep before our eyes—the fantasy that we should suffer no pain or loss. We need to replace this illusion with a clear view of reality—that to be alive on this planet means we will have loss and grief. Accepting these truths allows us to bear up under even the worst losses, and lays the important foundation stone of *reality,* which also helps us in the long haul of forgiving.

Accepting reality is incredibly important because the whole landscape of life can seem devastated in the wake of a serious offense and the crisis it causes.

For me, the harsh reality of visiting Herb in prison was not as miserable as his reality of living in prison—but it was hard enough to make me want to turn back on my commitment several times. After his release, we had to face a new kind of harshness. Because of Herb's high profile and the media's intensive coverage, he'd been branded in the eyes of almost everyone in our city. Because he'd pled guilty, there was no prolonged jury trial and the real facts never came out in public, leaving a false impression of Herb in everyone's mind. Consequently, there was also a false impression of "what kind of woman" I must be to "stand by a man like that." So it required amazing amounts of courage and dignity for both of us to hold our heads up in public. As I mentioned, our oldest daughter suffered humiliation in her graduate class. And even years after Herb's release from prison, when he and I collaborated on a book for parents, he was derided as a hypocrite and the publisher insisted I delete his valuable contributions.

When events seem "too much to bear," it triggers a desire to return to unforgiveness—unless we accept the fact that we are living in a new reality formed by the events. Acceptance tells us that the past is over, and the present and the future we once envisioned are not to be. Acceptance reminds us that this cannot be changed no matter how strongly we feel about it, or even if we could make the offender's life miserable. Accepting, and living in, reality keeps us from falling into an inner prison formed by those images of "what was" and "what might have been."

Learning to *bear up* under a new reality also requires you to accept that although you may forgive the offender and go on, others around you may not. They may resist, belittle, and even turn their backs.

Cheryl, whose brother's murderer went free, had to bear the virtual loss of her parents, who fell victim to bitterness and hatred, then crippling depression. Of course they remained in her life, but their emotional impairment was great. On occasion her mother would ask, bitterly, "How can you act so happy? Don't you even *care* that your brother is dead?" Once, when Cheryl spoke about forgiveness, her mother looked at her coldly and said, "Traitor."

Choosing to forgive can put us, strangely enough, at odds even with those who otherwise say they are for us. Mandy's mother and sister told her she was "stupid" for forgiving her ex-husband when he left her for another woman. Alex had to demand that his father call off his high-priced attorneys when they lost a malpractice trial against a doctor whose negligence left his son severely hearing-impaired. "Personally," Alex said, as his father pushed him to appeal, "I think your attorneys are keeping your emotions stirred up, and I don't believe them when they say they can win on appeal. I'm ready to forgive and move on. That's final."

It's true that friends and loved ones may believe we aren't acting in our own best interest when we want to forgive. They may decide we need to be "protected" from ourselves, shielded from future pain they imagine we'll suffer. This we must understand and accept, and we will need to set firm boundaries if we are going to stay the course of forgiveness.

Standing up for our choice to forgive, when others cannot, can be part of bearing up under a new reality. But learning to do so helps our forgiveness to become firm and effective over the long haul.

SEEKING "LIKE-MINDED" FRIENDS

As we've seen, the world and even other Christians may well interpret our desire to forgive as "weak," "overly spiritual," "codependent," or just plain "stupid." Strong as we may be, continuing to grow in forgiveness as we make it a life habit may also require us to find new support when our past support fails.

Jamie's mother refused to stop her bitter remarks after Jamie's husband, Barry, was convicted for repeatedly abusing their eight-year-old son. "Mother," Jamie said one day, "I can't have you around me like this. And I *demand* that you stop telling Paulie what a monster his father is. Barry is convicted and he's getting counseling. And Paulie and I need to forgive and heal. You can see us any time you want, but I can't have you grinding your heel in our wounds."

Jamie's mother eventually did comply, but in the meantime Jamie found support for herself and Paulie among friends in a county-sponsored support group and at church—support that helped them *live* forgiveness as a daily habit.

In my case, I was able to turn away from bitter and vocal detractors—even professional colleagues who denounced me behind my back—and to find focused, intentional support in my efforts to forgive. This support came mainly from Christian friends.

I found it especially supportive when several men let me know how important my acts of forgiveness were. Their remarks can be summed up like this: "I could have done what Herb did. But for the grace of God, that would be me."

It's not always effective to tune in only to those who say, out of hand, "I think you're doing the right thing." But when it comes to forgiving, having a supportive "amen chorus" around us is critical.

FOCUS ON HEALING AND REDEMPTION

As others choose to remain intently focused on the loss, forgiving for the long haul requires us to *stay open to the good that can come even from tragedy*. When we stay open to good, even if we must wait for it to be seen in time, we can experience healing and watch as our loss is redeemed.

Those who'd say, "No good can come from the loss or atrocity I've experienced," are—I mean this kindly—wrong. The question is, Will we *allow* good to come, and *watch* for it?

After our lives came apart, I didn't believe that good could come from our mess. There were obvious disasters staring us in the face. And moreover, when I began visiting Herb in prison, it seemed to me he only wanted to rehash the past. At first, I felt like the target of all his bitterness, anger, and blame. Seeing no good in this, I was only too ready to cut him off. Then it occurred to me that I'd complained for years that we didn't talk to each other. If there was no other good in this, we could begin talking again.

As I told you before, I had to set a healthy boundary—fifteen minutes of complaining—to keep from feeling wounded and misused. But I also decided that during those fifteen minutes I would not just defend myself against Herb's version of reality, or tune him out. I would *really* listen to him.

Opening myself like this allowed me to enter into Herb's head and heart, to see and feel the bitter events of our life from his vantage point. To my chagrin, I'd had little understanding of or empathy for him before, and I began to recognize how good it was that circumstances created this concentrated time in which we had nothing to do but enter into each other's hearts. To my greater chagrin, I saw myself through another's eyes—how I'd nagged and pouted. Seeing ourselves as we are, not as we want to see ourselves, may be uncomfortable, but it *always* does us good. I saw how much I needed to be forgiven, too.

Once I was alerted to look for good to come out of our circumstances, the picture changed. As events unfolded, both Herb and I began to focus on using our sins, mistakes, losses, and hurts for the good of others. In short, we began to see a redeeming purpose in what we'd been through.

Eventually, Herb learned to forgive himself—not an easy process for anyone—and because of that he is able to speak with authority, strength, and compassion to others who have made damaging mistakes.

The prison experience itself, *because* it was terrible and dehumanizing, gave Herb a tremendous compassion for prison inmates. During his incarceration, he had numerous opportunities to reach out to the profound needs of other men. He was not allowed to use his medical skills, of course, but he witnessed things that made him concerned about the lack of even substandard medical care—especially when he saw three relatively young prisoners die because of neglect and indifference by an inadequate medical staff.

Because of these major incidents and because of the daily mismanagement of medical care, Herb wrote to the Department of Justice in Washington, D.C. Because he was a physician, and because he was reasonable in the reporting, the Justice Department sent a Washington physician to verify his concerns. Following this, his name was given to the Law School of Washburn University in Topeka, Kansas, which was representing inmates at the prison in a class-action suit against the State of Kansas. Herb was chosen to testify before the federal judge who heard this case. It was a dramatic trial, and it resulted in an order requiring the state to provide adequate medical care for prisoners. Herb's testimony did not endear him to the state correctional system, but he took the risk.

While still in prison, Herb continued his own small ministry efforts. He wrote letters for men who couldn't write . . . read to those who were illiterate . . . listened as men talked out their anger, loneliness, and pain. He tutored many who wanted to learn. As he passed on the woes of inmates to family members in our support group, we found we could do much to heal and care for these desperate people. This book could be filled with stories that still break my heart—all because of the immense grace of practicing forgiveness daily.

I'm aware that some would not support humanitarian efforts on behalf of convicted felons. But we are not of that opinion. Rather, as a result of our redemptive focus, we began to see good come out of a bad circumstance.

For me, watching Herb come alive again, and be changed, was incredibly redemptive and supported my ongoing ability to forgive.

EMPATHY

Earlier, I talked about seeking information as a means of coming to an initial forgiveness. I want to return to our need to grow in understanding if forgiveness is to become our lifelong habit.

Learning to understand, or empathize with, your offender is the part of forgiveness that makes people crazy. This piece, together with the desire to see the other experience change and redemption, is what triggers the accusations of codependence.

To be clear, we are not seeking to understand or empathize in a weak-willed manner that condones. We do not take an attitude that leaves us saying, "There, there, you poor thing. I understand why you had to hurt me. I'll just overlook it." That is unbalanced and unhealthy indeed.

Rather, we empathize in order to understand our offenders' inner woundings, misunderstandings, and incorrect views about life and relating. We learn to stand in their shoes, to see life with their "givens" and from their viewpoints.

Personally, I believe this is what Jesus was doing, in part, when He spoke from the cross. With His back scourged open, and with nails pinning Him by wrists and ankles to wood beams, He said, "Father, forgive them, for they do not know what they are doing" (Luke 23:34). They did not know—but because He knew their hearts, Jesus understood. He'd looked into the open soul of humanity and seen their fear—that is, He understood how threatened they were by His authority and power and by His simple words that came as such a threat to their religious system.

Our prison talks taught me to listen to and learn about Herb. I learned a lot about him I'd never known when he was my husband. In time, thinking from his perspective, what he'd done made some sense. I can't say perfect sense, but enough. It convinced me I had to continue on this path of forgiveness by learning to make empathy a greater part of my life and our relationship.

RESTORATION

Herb returned from prison to live with the friend who'd offered him shelter some five years before, during our separation and divorce. My original intent in divorcing Herb was to totally leave him because I'd had enough heartache. Then my intent was to see him through this ordeal, then go our separate ways after his release. So it was with a bit of dismay that I realized what the process of forgiveness was leading toward. Thanks to our intense communication, and the deep level of openness and trust we discovered, we both realized love had returned. Not even the same kind of love we'd experienced early in our marriage, but a new love.

Undergoing therapy was, to say the least, abhorrent to Herb's pride. Yet he consented, after his release, to go through this in order to reorient himself to a society in which he had to make choices again and to work through the issues that had landed him in prison. Four years of life where you have no choice can be impairing.

We waited. Herb worked. And I watched. I saw a man even more lovable than the one I had married. He vowed he would never hurt me again. He was careful to keep me aware at all times of his whereabouts, who he was with, and what he was doing. For my part, I learned how to trust him again.

To remain in a forgiving attitude for the long haul does not require that the relationship be restored, or even that there be a face-to-face relationship at all. Emotional ties and emotional bondages exist whether or not two people ever see each other again. Unforgiveness, like codependency, keeps you linked in a negative bond forever, but forgiveness frees you whether or not you ever set eyes on the offender again.

What we can always work to restore, by building on the habit of forgiving, is our own inner balance and sanity, our peace with God, and grace toward others. When circumstances prevent us from physically looking an offender in the eye, achieving this type of personal restoration may require us to see the offender in our mind's eye and say, "I forgive you." This can be a powerful step in personal growth.

In our case, Herb and I were most definitely going to see each other again.

WHOEVER LOSES HIS LIFE . . .

Almost two years after his release from prison, Herb and I remarried. Like two silly teenagers, we went to a little town noted for a quick yet legal marriage. In a tiny Baptist chapel we repeated those age-old vows. We both knew this was best—and it was also fun! Our honeymoon was the return to our old home. Later, our children hosted a reception for us and our dearest, most loyal friends.

Rumors continued to hit me often—that I must be a truly sick person to have remarried this man. (Just for the record, I sought the best psychological evaluation I could find. No codependency was found.) I was able not only to survive the trauma of those years of stress, but to grow and continue to be productive. Once I'd recovered from the grief of those huge losses, I enjoyed life. To this day, I continually seek to cooperate with God to see good come out of so much bad.

Ultimately, what I discovered is the wisdom of a truth the world and those with a legalistic mindset will never understand. I learned what Jesus meant when He said, "Whoever loses his life for my sake will find it" (Matthew 10:39).

Herb and I have both come to understand the profound depths of this statement. Giving up our old ways of living—our resisting and retaliating—we found a new way to live that we'd never believed possible.

To continue to live in this new way requires a continual "losing" or "laying down" of our old ways in order to continually "win" by "taking up" the new way. Surely you can see that these events did not happen as they did because Grace and

Herb were great individuals. As you can tell, we were weak—sometimes even helpless—human beings.

And so we're learning, little by little, how to follow the path of forgiveness Jesus laid before us. By practicing a habit of forgiveness, gradually replacing the impulse to revenge, we're becoming witnesses to amazing redemptive work in our lives and the lives of others.

Isn't this what you want, too?

CHAPTER SEVEN

ETERNITY IN VIEW

PSYCHOLOGY HAS OFTEN BEEN SUSPECT IN THE MINDS OF biblically-centered Christians, and even seen as an enemy of faith. It's true, of course, that some psychologists have helped create this division by concluding that God is merely a "construct of the human mind," a projection created by our own minds— explaining away God as if He is only a sanctified version of the floating head of Oz. Some have also explained the human soul in merely rational terms, as if it were just some sort of ethereal, ghostly machine with a mechanical blueprint to figure out in order to understand and "modify" our reactions.

Faced with this reductionist treatment of God and humanity, people of faith have not only rightly rejected these psychologists' views, but have often gone a step further and rejected—or at least held as suspect—psychology itself. Too frequently, sincere and faithful Christian psychologists hear their God-given calling attacked and ridiculed from pulpits on Sunday morning.

So far, we've looked at forgiveness in a way that combines and applies Jesus' profound and beautiful teachings to the spiritual and psychological responses triggered in us when we're hurt, attacked, and offended. In a sense, we've looked inside the human mind and soul a bit mechanistically, and done so for three reasons.

First, Jesus' teachings on forgiveness, as we noted, are often viewed (and taught) through the legalistic mindset, turning them into a higher set of "immutable laws" that become impossible for everyday people to live up to. They are actually an invitation to rest in grace and personal forgiveness, which makes forgiving others possible. Second, "slowing down" our reactions by studying them step by step makes gaining control of them, with God's help, possible—and self-control is a fruit of the Spirit that too often eludes sincere Christians who want to change their behavior. Third, seeing Jesus' teaching on judgment and forgiveness *in light of these interior reactions* creates a greater sense of awe for His insights into our soul. Is the Creator of the human soul not able to understand its workings?

We took some pains to lace together Jesus' teachings on forgiveness with the mechanics of our inner reactions because they are wonderfully compatible and awe-inspiring. Taken together, they offer us the hope of really changing—not merely talking about our need to forgive, or wishing we *could* forgive, but giving us a divine motivation, the hope, and the means to grow in the forgiving nature of God.

Yet there is another perspective, another dimension, we want to bring to our understanding of forgiveness. That is the eternal perspective.

If we as Christians believe our soul is immortal, and if we believe—as Jesus also taught—that we will step out of this life into eternity and witness an eternal judgment, then there's an even greater urgency in His teaching about forgiveness. This, of course, is where the man and woman of faith step apart from the unbelieving person. This is where we are asked to take a leap of faith—to step away from the study of soul mechanics and into the realm of God's revelation to us about our future.

Put simply, if we believe what Jesus showed us about the

world to come, we find an even greater reason to live free of past hurts by letting go of offenses—forever—and to accept His invitation to work along with Him to free others, if possible, from the results of their own harmful acts.

WE'RE GOING TO LIVE FOREVER

The prophet Isaiah foretold that Jesus would "open eyes that are blind" (42:7). Isaiah was not only referring to the miracles of Jesus in which physical eyes would be healed, but also to the restoration of our spiritual sight—that is, a more accurate vision of God, how He treats us as His children, and the future that lies ahead for us. When Jesus revealed God to us as a "heavenly Father," He fulfilled Isaiah's prophecy by transforming humanity's vision of the God who made us and who we will one day face again.

One way that Jesus opened our spiritual vision was to establish that there will come a day when every one of us must stand before God. Consider His teaching, as recorded by Matthew. Jesus told His disciples:

> "When the Son of Man comes in his glory, and all the angels with him, he will sit on his throne in heavenly glory. All the nations will be gathered before him, and he will separate the people one from another as a shepherd separates the sheep from the goats. He will put the sheep on his right and the goats on his left." (25:31-33)

These words create a powerful image in our minds about the reckoning to come for all of us when we stand before Jesus face to face in eternity. The apostle John records a similar scene, which Jesus showed him in the Spirit, and by revelation, late in John's life:

> Then I saw a great white throne and him who was seated on it. Earth and sky fled from his presence, and there was

no place for them. And I saw the dead, great and small,
standing before the throne, and books were opened.
Another book was opened, which is the book of life. The
dead were judged according to what they had done as
recorded in the books. (Revelation 20:11-12)

Jesus gave us a powerful image of the judgment to come! He
surely meant for us to internalize this image, to carry it with us
in our heads and hearts at all times. If we meditate on this image
of the coming judgment, it begins to work powerfully in us.

Primarily, living with the reality that there is a judgment to
come helps us to relax and find inner peace for ourselves. Cheryl
was able to experience peace when her brother's murderer
walked free after this world's justice system twice failed to bring
the man to accountability. Likewise, Bruce was able to live
beyond turmoil and agitation when he confronted his uncle who
had abused him sexually many times as a boy—only to have his
uncle reply, with a deadpan look, "It's all in your head—nothing
like that ever happened." Leonard was wrongly accused of
molesting children in a daycare center, sent to prison for
seventeen years, and seen as a monster by his community and
many of his old friends—and even though the child and her
family later recanted, saying they were pushed by a county
prosecutor to "trump up" accusations, much of Leonard's life
was wrecked. Even so, Cheryl, Bruce, and Leonard have found
inner rest and strength in meditating on Jesus' descriptions of the
judgment that those who wronged them will *have* to face one
day in a "higher court."

It's important to note the wonderful favor Jesus did for us, in
practical and psychological terms, when He parted the veil of time
and allowed us to see ahead into the future.

At a human level, every one of us is created to need
something called *closure* in relation to the people and events in
our lives. This means simply that when an action, conversation,

or event has begun—especially one that affects us greatly or puts our sense of well-being into turmoil—we need to know that the energy and pressure of the force against us will be stopped. We feel this need subtly, for instance, when conversations are left dangling, when a chore is left unfinished, and more acutely when a serious wrong has been done to us. Beyond the need to see the open-ended things "finished up" or "stopped," we also have an innate need to know that wrongs will be righted, that things put out of balance will be balanced again. This need will lead us to a second look at the talionic impulse, that inner force that drives us to seek revenge, in a moment.

Jesus knew, of course, what a fallen, broken, imperfect world He had stepped into in order to teach us. Here, the righting, rebalancing, and justice is very far from perfect. Boys and girls are affected for life by terrible emotional and physical abuses. Murderers go free. Innocent people are thrown in jail, ostracized, and see their lives ruined.

What Jesus did by giving us images of the judgment to come was this: He gave us reason to let go of our insistence on seeing justice here and now—to relax our natural need for closure—and to rest in the faith that justice *will* be done later.

At the end of this age, God will right all wrongs. And then He will say to us, as a new, recreated heaven and earth are born before our eyes, "Behold, I make all things new!" (Revelation 21:5, KJV).

In this new world, Cheryl and her brother will greet each other again, never to be apart. Bruce's broken heart and many shed tears will be healed and dried forever. Leonard will be entirely free from the shadows of accusation, with a new life opening before him.

Jesus blessed us with the knowledge that *what is lost to us in this life will be restored in the next*. And yet, giving us this view of the future is meant to do something more than bring rest and peace to our souls. The restoration of things lost to us is just one side of the picture.

WHATSOEVER YOU DO TO THE LEAST . . .

After helping the disciples to envision God's separation of the sheep and the goats, Jesus went on to tell them:

> "Then the King will say to those on his right, 'Come, you who are blessed by my Father; take your inheritance, the kingdom prepared for you since the creation of the world. For I was hungry and you gave me something to eat, I was thirsty and you gave me something to drink, I was a stranger and you invited me in, I needed clothes and you clothed me, I was sick and you looked after me, I was in prison and you came to visit me." (Matthew 25:34-36)

Now Jesus—in the parable, the "King"—is speaking to them about their good works. And the people in the parable ask Him, wonderingly, "When did we do all these things?"

Jesus tells them—and He tells us, His followers today— "Whatever you did for one of the least of these brothers of mine, you did for me" (25:40).

Reading this passage, we're reminded of two things:

First, that Jesus is the good Shepherd who has gone out to seek the lost sheep, including the offenders of the world (see John 10:14). To the self-righteous, who judged Him for befriending "sinners," He said it was not the "healthy" who needed His soul-restoring work, but the "sick." And so it's no stretch to recognize that the sick and the prisoners He refers to are not only the physically ill and those in cells of cement and steel. He includes the spiritually sick and those imprisoned and separated from God and humanity by the guilt of their sins and wrongdoing. Jesus refers *even to these sick and guilty offenders* as "my brothers"—and speaks in the same forgiving spirit as when He identified with us in our guilt and sin.

In powerful words we cannot avoid, Jesus has not only

reminded us again not to judge offenders, but taught us that on this side of eternity and until God says otherwise, *we are to see them as potential brothers and sisters in His kingdom.*

Second, Jesus reminds us—*Whatever you do for them, you do for me*—that He counts our efforts toward these people as something of a personal favor to Him. Why? Because when we reach out to the lost offenders of the world we're cooperating with Him in His work, which is to seek every one of these people in order to heal their soul diseases and bring them into the eternal kingdom of His Father. We cooperate with Him by having in us the same forgiving spirit that prompted Jesus to enter into this fallen, hurtful, unjust world.

There is something important here for us as believers—something perhaps related to our own eternal destiny. Jesus may be saying something about the difference between the everyday work we do to make our daily bread in this world and the redeeming work we do at His side as preparation for life in God's eternal new world.

Let's return to the image of our future, given to us in John's revelation. Here we see ourselves—even as believers, knowing Jesus has already purchased our eternity in heaven—standing before God awaiting judgment:

> . . . and books were opened. Another book was opened,
> which is the book of life. The dead were judged according
> to what they had done as recorded in the books. (Revelation
> 20:12)

Imagine that you are called to stand before God. You step up, and humbly kneel. The "book of life" is checked—and *in Jesus' own script, your name is written there!* Can you imagine what gratitude, joy, and relief you'll experience?

And then the *other* book is checked—the book that records the events of your life. Not only the events, but the way you *responded* to these events, along with your other deeds and actions. This, apparently, is the same book revealed to the psalmist when he wrote, "All the days ordained for me were written in your book before one of them came to be" (Psalm 139:16).

Suddenly, you see the big picture of your life and understand the great truth Jesus was trying to tell us in His parable about the sheep and the goats: *God sovereignly, providentially, arranged all the events of your life—allowing even the offenses!—in order to help involve you with Him in His work of seeking and redeeming the lost offenders.*

In a flash, you recognize the simple genius of this whole plan. In another moment, you will be admitted to eternity, there to be rejoined with loved ones you lost, there to start a whole new life, in a recreated world. What was lost to you *temporarily* in the fallen world you've left behind will be restored *eternally.* And even the offenses against you were part of a prethought plan—God's plan to give you a deeply vested interest in helping Him in His work of building a kingdom of eternal peace out of a whole world of people who are bent on hurting, and retaliating against, each other.

The question before you—before each one of us—is this: *What will the book of our life say we did in response to the events God allowed to be written into the "plot" of our lives? What will it say we did in response to Jesus' "brothers" who offended and harmed us?*

OUR WORK IN THE KINGDOM

It's doubtful that many of us would involve ourselves much, or very deeply, in God's true redemptive work, especially with those we consider the "worst of the worst," unless He allowed a motivating factor to occur in our lives. That "motivating factor" seems to be the offenses committed against us. The truth is, offenses—especially those that we find so impossible to forgive—bind us in some way to the offender. Either we are bound together in an ongoing story where our motivation is anger and retaliation, or one in which our motivation is to forgive and to become free from penalty.

There are two important points to make here: First, we must remember that it is not our job to be certain that everyone in our life comes to Christ and experiences salvation. It isn't in our power, ultimately, to change people's hearts. Sometimes Christians have been pressured and manipulated with the idea that the eternal destiny of others rests on their shoulders. This thinking creates a Christian type of codependency—as if we are solely responsible for the eternal destiny and happiness of the people in our lives.

We do have a "task," though, and that is *to witness to the forgiveness and freedom offered by God by freely offering forgiveness.* Though we aren't *responsible* for another's choices or eternal destiny, we can *influence* it by demonstrating with our lives how real God's love and mercy are to us. We can live in a way that makes others want to know this generous love as genuinely and deeply as we know it.

This, at least, is how we can enter into our co-labor with Christ as we begin, here and now, to work at building God's eternal kingdom.

Second, the descriptions Jesus gave us of the coming judgment may tell us something not only about our co-labor with Christ here, but perhaps in the *hereafter* as well.

We could well ask: If our entrance into God's eternal kingdom is guaranteed by our faith in Christ's sacrifice of blood that purchased our redemption, why are we to be judged on the basis of our works? Is it to make us feel bad for the times we've failed to obey God, or to assign us an eternal residence in a lesser neighborhood of heaven while God's more obedient followers get "mansions"?

There is another possibility, and though any guess at what eternity will be like is speculation, it's worth considering.

What if God's "judgment" of us as believers is the time when the works we've done in Jesus' name are scrutinized—almost the way a resume is studied—and our place and work in God's re-created world is determined? If that's the case, we'll be "judged" by our works in the sense that our works demonstrate exactly what it is we're suitable and prepared to do. Then we would find our place in eternity based on the work of God that our compassionate heart has already found its joy in doing. (Read Matthew 25:31-36 again with this thought in mind.)

We do not know what this new world, free of the curse, will be like or what work there will be for us, but it's doubtful God has it in mind for us to sit around on clouds, playing harps forever and ever! As noted, the scenario we describe is speculative, but it's a possibility worth consideration.

For now, we must look at an immediate question: How can these images of the eternal world to come make any real difference now?

BECOMING SINGLE-MINDED

The way we look at reality determines a lot about the way we act. It's very easy for us to focus on events in the here and now, especially painful events that form such powerful images in our memories. These real events remain in our mind's eye, sometimes causing even strong physiological effects in our bodies as we almost literally relive the event. Thinking of an offender's abuse, neglect, or betrayal, we can feel our pulse quicken, our breathing go shallow, and our muscles tense, all in response to the blast of adrenaline that memory has triggered our body to release! Physically, we're as ready to lash out, or flee from danger, as if the offense were happening right now. It's hard to feel forgiveness at too deep a level when our body is tense, anxious, and ready to strike.

What we've just described is the power one set of mental images—negative ones—has to prevent us from letting go of the past. We're stuck with all the negative effects of unforgiveness.

On the other hand, cultivating the eternal perspective by fixing our thoughts on eternal realities that lie ahead can have an equally strong effect on us for good. Splicing Jesus' "footage" of the future onto the end of every negative event we think about is a powerful antidote to unforgiveness and bitterness—spirit-lifting indeed! No wonder the apostle Paul encouraged us several times to set our minds on things above (see Colossians 3:2).

If we do not cultivate this new perspective—seeing temporal events as having their culmination in eternal realities—we are pretty much guaranteed to experience the unsteady, unpleasant life of what James calls the "double-minded" believer (1:2-8).

Allan experienced the unhappy roller-coaster ride of double-mindedness, along with the stress it brings. Holly, his wife, was pressured by her boss to lift and move heavy boxes, even though she was nearing her third trimester of pregnancy. She and Allan were living near poverty, and this job offered them the maternity insurance they needed. When her boss threatened to let her go if she didn't pitch in, Holly went against her better judgment, resulting in a serious internal injury. Within a week she miscarried and, to make things worse, learned that her injuries made it impossible to bear another child.

Holly's grief, added to his own anger, sent Allan's stress level and his blood pressure skyrocketing. He was serious about his faith and tried to forgive Holly's boss, who now denied he'd "threatened and forced" her into the heavy lifting. Allan could forgive the man, recognizing the failings and petty greed of an unbelieving man who needed God in his life. But every time Allan saw a daddy playing in the park with his little child, grief overcame him, and then rage. Sometimes he wanted to hurt, even kill, the man he saw during those moments as "nothing but a monster." These seesawing emotions were tearing Allan to pieces.

Is it any wonder, even when we face lesser offenses, that double-mindedness is a condition James urges us to resolve?

The hurdle most of us will face is the fact that seeing things from a spiritual perspective is just not natural to us. The ability to see, hear, smell, and feel threat is instinctive in us. But viewing life from the eternal perspective needs to be cultivated. Otherwise, our old, habitual way of responding remains strong within us. We tend to act like Christians when things are all right, then forget "all that spiritual stuff" and turn vengeful the second an event, or even the memory of it, overwhelms our weak faith.

The cable network Court TV recently featured a father whose son was accused of murdering his wife. He was sure his son was "framed," while the young woman's parents were convinced the young man was guilty, though there was no firm evidence of this. Once they'd accepted him as a son; now that vision of him was obliterated by anger and grief. They wanted to see him die in the electric chair or by lethal injection.

You could see the sad confusion on the face of the young man's father as he was interviewed. He and his wife were also devastated by their daughter-in-law's murder and wanted to find the killer. Moreover, the four in-laws had been close friends, but now the girl's parents had rejected them and made them opponents in a sad, bitter struggle.

"I'm praying to forgive them for what they're doing to [my son]," he said, sadly. "But to do so would be like saying, 'It's *okay* for you to want my son to die.'"

The anguish caused by harsh temporal realities does make it harder for us to see beyond our hurt—harder, *but by no means impossible.*

How, then, do we end our own inner struggle and become single-minded? How can we focus our own spirit into a solid determination to cooperate with God in a way that sets us free within and offers His grace to our offenders?

The answer we offer is to develop our "spiritual sight" through the practice of biblical meditation, until we have made it our habit to live with eternity in view no matter how difficult the earthly realities that face us.

Meditation is an ancient spiritual discipline long practiced by the Hebrews, and later by Christians. The psalms, among other Scriptures, are the products of meditations by godly people *and* are wonderful aids to us. We refer to meditation as a *spiritual dis-*

cipline because it is a means of training our inner person to develop and become strong in its focus on godly things. Like any discipline, it takes time and practice.

There is an important distinction to be made here: We are not advocating meditation in the Eastern manner, which is an attempt to negate, empty, or erase the self in order to become "nothing." Eastern meditation has as its goal union with oblivion. Nor are we advocating meditation in the new age manner, which is an attempt to focus one's latent energies enough to shape reality or create a new reality, or to draw "spiritual entities" to oneself. The goal of Christian meditation is not to experience the so-called "bliss" of nirvana and oblivion, or to gain control of mystical powers that lead to the forbidden practice of magic or witchcraft.

Christian meditation has as its goal these things: *first* to gain a strong, clear understanding of God, His will, and His work; *second*, to unite our will and personal strength to God's will and strength so that we are obediently cooperating with Him in fulfilling His purposes. We focus the united strength of our whole being—mind, body, and spirit—to fulfill a prayer we've prayed so often: "May your will be done on earth as it is in heaven— through me!" (see Matthew 6:10).

Meditation, as a means of making the eternal perspective real to us, is not difficult. Let's take a look at how it works.

THE PRACTICE OF MEDITATION

Meditative thinking is something we actually do all the time. Meditation is really the simple practice of going over and over a thought or image, "feeding" on it in a way that's been likened to a cow chewing its cud. So it's important to begin by taking stock of what it is we're feeding our soul, as we prepare to fill our minds with biblical thoughts and images.

This usually leads to the discovery that we need to do some mental "house cleaning." We do that by prayerfully asking God to help us listen to our own self-talk and to be aware of mental images that will prevent us from developing a healthy mindset.

When we really tune in to what we're thinking, we might find thoughts like these:

I'll forgive when and if . . .
If I forgive, he'll have to . . .
If I forgive, God, You'll have to . . .
I'll trust You, God, to see that justice is done. But if You don't . . .

It's easy for us to want forgiveness and understanding for ourselves, while our attitude of forgiveness toward others is conditional. This conditional thinking will get in the way when we try to fix our hearts on godly thoughts and images.

Or we might play and replay fantasies in which we see ourselves insulting or harming the offender. These can occur in our waking moments, or in dreams, and can be quite violent.

Though she insisted she wanted to forgive, Sara kept envisioning her husband getting injured in a car wreck after he left her for a gay man. She'd say "jokingly" to friends, "I don't want to see him dead—just maimed." Eventually, she had to face up to the reality that in her bitterness she wanted to see her ex-husband physically harmed because of the painful sense of rejection he'd dealt her.

Philip dreamed many nights that he'd beaten to death the man who'd coaxed his eleven-year-old daughter into a van and brutally molested her.

The discovery of conditional self-talk and even violent images doesn't prove we're bad Christians. It proves we're normal human beings.

The first step we need to take is to confess our thoughts to God, or to a pastor, counselor, or spiritual friend. We can tell them about our decision to mentally "clean house" in order to move on to a better place in our meditative thinking. And like the man who said to Jesus, "I believe, but help me in my *unbelief!*" we may need to pray, *I choose to forgive, but help me when my thoughts are unforgiving.*

Getting honest about our own inner condition allows us to begin to gain self-control, which is important to support the *supernatural* path of faith we're taking. Then we can begin to transform the very thoughts and images that the old impulse to revenge has turned loose.

In Grace's case this meant that, though she said she wanted to forgive Herb, in the back of her mind she continued to envision an "escape hatch." It was small and hidden, and it represented an attitude she greatly downplayed in her conscious thinking: *If things don't work out with Herb, if he doesn't change very much, I can always leave him.*

Praying one day, however, it seemed that God made her focus on the escape hatch she was trying to conceal in the back of her mind. With God's help, she saw it for what it was—a symbol of double-mindedness and instability. This gave her the power to choose not merely to close the escape hatch, but to replace it in her thinking altogether.

The second step we need to take, as we eliminate old thinking, is to cultivate new thinking.

Certainly we can begin by focusing on Scripture. Here are just a few important verses that have a powerful effect within as we turn them over in our minds. It can be of further benefit to modify and personalize them, as several have been here:

> Lord, you are good, and ready to forgive. (Psalm 86:5)

> If I forgive, I will be forgiven. (Luke 6:37)

> Forgive my sins, for I also forgive everyone who sins against me. (Luke 11:4)

> God, for Christ's sake, has forgiven me. (Ephesians 4:23)

We can also help ourselves along by looking for simple images from everyday life that can speak deeply in the symbolic language of the soul. Some of us who are more intuitive find that this type of meditation also helps to replace hurt and angry feelings with feelings of release and forgiveness.

Grace recalls asking her mother to teach her how to do needlework on bleached cloth from a flour sack, a common thing during the Depression. Some fine stitchery, and there was a beautiful pillowcase or towel. With a little girl's excitement, she began to stitch the bright blue, rose, and yellow thread into a simple pattern—and with a little girl's impatience, she also soon gave up. What began as a dream of achievement ended as a symbol of failure and shame. Blocking her mother's attempts to get her to finish, she tangled the threads, got it dirty, and then "lost" it.

But Grace's mother saw a chance to teach her something. She searched for and found the piece of cloth, washed it, corrected the mistakes, and made Grace finish it. She then made a pillow for the sofa in the front room. When visitors admired it, she nodded and said how proud she was of this piece she and Grace had made "together."

To Grace, the story and the pillow form simple but strong images of forgiveness and redemption. She recalls her mother's search for the lost article that shame had concealed, how she washed the dirty stains out, her patience in untangling Grace's mess, and her creativity in making something beautiful out of "failed" efforts.

It's easy to see how this wonderful story is rich in meanings that speak deeper than language and straight to the soul. In our mind's eye we can imagine God, working in the eternal dimension to seek us, untangle our messes, create something wonderful from our lives, and even to take pride in us, who He—amazingly!—refers to as His own children (see 1 John 3:1).

Perhaps the most powerful images we can meditate on are those of the coming day of judgment that Scripture depicts.

David finds that these images have great potency in

cultivating his ability to take the eternal perspective when wrongs are done to him.

Several years ago, an international Christian ministry hired David to develop books for them. Not long into the relationship, he realized far more was being asked of him than the written agreement specified. He agreed to continue working for the ministry, provided they would renegotiate fairer financial terms in light of the extra work. Many thousands of dollars were at stake. A woman who was high up in the ministry agreed to David's terms.

Months went by, and renegotiations were stalled by one "crisis" after another. In good faith, believing this Christian woman would be true to her word, David kept working. As time moved on, he, naturally, began to press the issue. The ministry's reasons for asking to delay the renegotiation were plausible at first: The ministry was under extreme financial pressure; then the staff was moving to a new building; then the head of the ministry was reported to be having "health problems." By the time David realized he was being strung along, he was tens of thousands of dollars in the hole.

When David finally insisted that the contract be redrawn, he was summarily terminated. Because the terms of renegotiation had been discussed in private and there were no witnesses, he had no documentation to prove the woman had made verbal agreements that would be legally binding.

Stunned, David realized he'd been intentionally manipulated by the head of a Christian ministry. The money he'd lost, because of lies, was money he'd counted on for his children's college education. His services, along with his children's money, were essentially stolen.

"My oldest son is headed for college next year," says David. "And every time I look at the small amount I have set aside, knowing I got so little for all my hard work, I can begin to relive the offense. The frustration and anger can get pretty raw and intense if I let it.

"That's when I have to take the long view of things.

"I remind myself that God is the judge, and not me. I release this woman into His hands, and say, 'I don't hold this charge against her.' In my mind's eye, I see her standing before the judgment seat, while God opens the book of her life.

"To be honest, when I first tried this I was praying in the back of my mind, *Get her, God.*

"Then I realized something. If I was standing behind her watching—*I was next in line!* Now, I've never treated anyone with such calculating coldness. But I couldn't be a hypocrite or a fool. I began to pray, *God, I don't know how You'll sort this out, but I know You're both fair and merciful. I have to believe You'll be just and loving to both of us.*

"For me, this is transforming. It's also like pressing the 'pause' button and halting this particular drama in my life. Even though there is no openness on the part of this ministry to negotiate a fair settlement, I can let it go and rest inside, knowing it's in God's hands.

"The most amazing thing about meditating on this image," says David, "is that knowing God will open the book of my life, too, totally transforms my attitude.

"As I think about this woman standing before God, and me next in line, I find myself praying, *'Be merciful in Your judgment, Father, and loving in Your correction.'*"

PRACTICE, PRACTICE

Developing the ability to see our lives from the eternal perspective is part of the long haul of forgiveness. For that reason, we will need to give ourselves time to work it into our thought patterns, and then into our souls. We can do this by practicing regularly the discipline of meditation.

This, we believe, is what James meant in part when he told us to "persevere" in faith in the same passage in which he warned against double-mindedness. By daily practice, and good old-fashioned perseverance, we replace old thought patterns and images of vengeance with new thoughts about forgiveness and mercy.

In time, this renewed mind takes hold, and the eternal perspective becomes a reality in us. God's presence seems nearer; heaven presses close. Gradually, our practice of forgiving becomes second nature—or, rather, "new nature" in us.

It's true—as Christians, eternal life is ours. But the choice to live free in spirit as "immortals" or as unhappy children of earth is also ours.

The literary giant John Milton said, "The mind can make a heaven of hell, or a hell of heaven," understanding the needless torments we put ourselves through, when peace and spiritual freedom can be ours. And Augustine said, "Our souls are restless, Lord, until we find our rest in thee."

From what we have presented here, our hope is that you will understand how important it is to live in light of heaven—empowered by an eternal perspective—when you need to forgive, and live free.

CHAPTER EIGHT

FORGIVING YOURSELF

UP TO THIS POINT, WE'VE BEEN FOCUSED OUTWARD, LOOKING AT WHAT it takes to forgive when someone has caused us great harm. Now we need to consider what is for many of us an *unexpected* aspect of forgiveness

As the habit of forgiving deepens and takes hold in us, we begin to see how much *we* are in need of forgiveness.

"Forgive, and you will be forgiven" is a teaching that has little meaning for us as long as we continue to insist that we really don't need to be forgiven "as much as" the one who's wronged us. Thinking this way demonstrates the legalistic, judging/measuring mindset. Some phrases you may discover in your thinking and conversation are a dead giveaway of this attitude:

Sure, I've done things wrong. I've sinned. But not like that.

Yes, I'm sure I've hurt people—but never *intentionally*.

I was in a bad place at the time. I didn't mean to. But you have to understand that . . .

These statements are indications of *comparing, minimizing,* and *rationalizing* or *excusing*. They reveal that we all avoid taking responsibility, which is the foundation of mature behavior in our relationships with God, others, and ourselves.

Yet as forgiveness becomes a lively impulse within us, it begins to have a "collateral" effect—that is, it begins to work in other ways than we first intended or imagined. In the beginning, we set out to find resolution and peace from the wrongs others have done. At some point, it's as if we're staring into a mirror, seeing ourselves in need of forgiveness, too.

The impulse we meet in ourselves now is the impulse to *defend,* to *justify,* to *avoid*. Others set out to do harm. We don't try to harm others! Even if we do wrong, it is unintentional. Or it's not "as bad as" what others do. This is called *blocking the truth*— and as long as we do it, we are not growing. In fact, if we persist in blocking the truth about ourselves, the stress and anxiety that result will erode the peace we had found. Suddenly, this business about forgiveness is frustrating again, and the process is thrown into reverse.

So there is bad news and good news about forgiveness. At some point we'll face our own need for forgiveness and enter into a pitched battle in defense of our own goodness and intentions. The good news is that if we recognize the battle as the resistance of the legalistic mindset fighting for life, and if we face our own need to be forgiven, we overcome a major hurdle in our move toward spiritual health and maturity.

BUT . . . BUT . . .

Grace meted out some stern discipline when her daughter Kathy was little and picked flowers from a neighbor's garden without permission. Coming down on the side of "teaching her a lesson," Grace now admits her correction for this action was "major overkill." A gentler manner and a more thoughtful response would have made a good impression on Kathy, whom Grace knew to be a sensitive, obedient child. The neighbor, at least, was gracious when the teary, trembling, ponytailed little girl stood alone at her front door, confessing to her crime. Years later, when Kathy was an adult and could talk about the intense pain and shame she'd felt, Grace recognized that her manner of discipline had been deficient in *compassionate training* and was therefore out of balance. Even years later, she continues to work at forgiving herself for past incidents like this.

David went through a four-year life upheaval involving major stressors like a job change and the loss of a parent to cancer, drawing his focus and energy from the needs of his teenaged sons and preteen daughter. When a friend casually observed how "self-absorbed" he'd become, he realized why he sensed an empty gap between himself and his children. And he felt a wave of guilt and regret that four years of mentoring, closeness, and the old fun they'd had before were lost and gone. Forgiving himself requires patience and work.

Candidly, we have found ourselves confronted by sin and failure and wanted to crouch behind that first line of defense when accusations fly at us like bullets. We've observed the objections rising: *But I didn't know better . . . But I didn't mean to . . . But at the time I couldn't have done otherwise.* This is stark evidence, of course, of mankind's oldest tendency, which is to feel shame and to hide from the truth and personal accountability. In ourselves we recognize this tendency to dodge the truth, and we overcome it by admitting we've done wrong. But letting ourselves off the hook can be another matter.

If we know God has forgiven us, why is forgiving ourselves so hard?

When we admit we've wronged another, we have to look at the consequences of our actions and choices. We face the fact that others have paid a dear cost because, as one Christian liturgy puts it, "we have sinned in what we have done and in what we have failed to do." This can be excruciating, when the one you've harmed is—in the ironic nature of human reality—also someone for whom you'd give your very life! But then, to be human is to have a mature view that recognizes the mixture of settled facts and contradictions we are.

Daily, we face the need to grow in grace and forgiveness for ourselves if we are to follow Jesus' path toward maturity.

SHAME AND PRIDE

One reason it's so hard to forgive ourselves is that sometimes our own hurtful words and actions don't even make sense to us! We can feel Paul's confusion and frustration when he wrote, "What I do is not the good I want to do" (Romans 7:19). How can we have hurt loved ones when we knew better, never wanted to hurt them, and actually wanted good for them?

Another reason we resist forgiving ourselves is that we can hold unreasonably high standards for ourselves. In short, we demand perfection for ourselves, and don't allow for a learning curve. This can be especially hard for Christians who have been taught to "Be perfect [or "whole"], therefore, as your heavenly Father is perfect" (Matthew 5:48). But this is actually a statement about the inner growth we can experience as we allow God to bring together the scattered, disunited impulses within us into a mature, focused unity. And so, immature "perfectionism" works against us, keeping us both from learning and from graceful maturity.

Underneath our difficulty with forgiving ourselves lies one of humanity's core issues: *shame.*

Much has been written about shame by both secular and Christian psychologists—shame being defined as a deep and painful sense of "defectiveness" that causes us discomfort. But if we stare long enough into the face of shame, we discover that it is the reverse side of something else, and that is *pride.* Today, our tendency is to want to "heal" shame, which is a wise thing to do if by that we mean showing shame to be what it is—something that older Christian wisdom recognized as *wounded self-love.*

Armed with this understanding, we can see in our resistance, even refusal, to forgive ourselves a prideful self-love that makes it excruciating to see and accept imperfection in ourselves. *We can't be imperfect! We just won't have it!* But it's so.

A pastor berates himself bitterly when he recognizes that his counsel actually harmed someone in his congregation. For weeks he subjects himself to a mental lashing. *These people are counting on me. How could I be so stupid?* He may consider punishing himself by leaving the ministry. Or he may judge himself unfit or impaired, and stop offering counseling. Shame, or wounded self-love, is behind these impulses—when forgiveness could help him ask self-assessing questions like, *How can I improve my counseling skills?*

A Christian woman discovers her gossip has hurt a close friend. She goes through similar bouts of self-judgment and self-punishing thoughts. Getting beyond wounded self-love could allow her space for self-assessment, too. She could ask, *Why did I need to use insider information to appear "in the know" in another's eyes?*

If we seek our reflection in a mirror that can only show us our good side, we will never see the self that—because of God's love for us—deserves our patient attention. Therefore, we'll never be able to address sins and flaws that hurt others and need correction.

GUILT OVERLOAD

Another reason we have a hard time forgiving ourselves is that the skill of *self-assessment* has been crippled. This can happen in childhood, or in adulthood, when we place too much trust in another person's assessment of us and that assessment is harsh or overly critical.

In short, we develop self-blaming tendencies. Carrying the weight of guilt feels too normal, and forgiving ourselves too abnormal.

For many of us, this tendency to carry a guilt overload developed in childhood. Perhaps we had parents who, in a well-intended effort to teach right values, inflicted guilt on us instead. Certain approaches to Christianity can make us feel like everything we do is either a good or bad "witness." And because we're human and prone to fail, we can often appear to be "poor witnesses for Christ." *This is not to discredit the concept of being a witness.* But we are witnesses to what we have seen, or known to be deeply true—and we cannot be "good witnesses for Christ" when we've experienced the heaping on of guilt by those who apparently do not know how to help others experience the living hope that is ours in Christ (see Colossians 1:27).

On a more general level, many of us were too critically assessed by teachers, coaches, older relatives and siblings, or neighbors, and took their judgment as the gospel truth about ourselves. They may have used words like *always* and *never:* "You'll never be responsible." "I can never trust you the way I can trust your sister." These sentences "sentence" us to live with a spirit that picks up guilt and blame the way black clothing picks up lint!

Still others overtenderized us by blaming us for *their* problems: "Your father wouldn't be irritable all the time if you weren't such a poor student." "I drink because I have to work so hard to support all you kids."

These influences weaken our ability to recognize what responsibility is ours and what belongs to someone else. Everything must be, in some way, "our fault."

Randy could not forgive himself for his mother's death from leukemia. For a long time, his counselor couldn't find the root of his illogical acceptance of this guilt. As they talked, though, it gradually came clear.

As a small boy, Randy had been truly mischievous and often made extra work and worry for his hard-working mother. Her most oft-repeated phrase was, "Randy, you're going to be the death of me someday!" When he was not quite twelve, his mother was diagnosed with leukemia. She lived a few months in misery and then died. Believing he'd murdered his own mother, Randy couldn't forgive himself—and, consequently, couldn't forgive anyone else in his life.

When we have no true sense of the magnitude of an offense—how can we when it's not really related to something we did?—we will remain guilt-ridden. With nothing real to gauge by, how can you know when *enough* guilt is enough? For that matter, then, how do you know when someone else's sadness over hurting you is enough? How can you let someone else off the hook, when you're dangling uncertainly on it yourself?

Recognizing a tendency to take on guilt that is not ours, and the habit of self-blame, is a healthy step toward forgiving ourselves.

Continuing to punish ourselves—referring to ourselves as "worms," "losers," "stupid," "bad," "evil"—keeps us imprisoned in an unhealthy self-focus. We never face the work of cooperating with God in discovering the specific roots of our weakness, and accepting responsibility to work with Him to achieve change and mature growth.

Whatever the reasons may be for failing to forgive ourselves, self-forgiveness *is* a necessary step in our spiritual maturity.

LESSONS FROM A VET ON SELF-FORGIVENESS

Herb, whose story we have related earlier, has learned about the need for self-forgiveness. So far, we've presented his experience from Grace's perspectives. Here, we believe it's valuable to have him relate his experience and wisdom on this subject himself.

Herb's Perspective

When you come to see yourself as the person who, by his own actions, has caused pain and anguish to others, forgiving yourself can seem very difficult. Yet it's important because it's the first step in reestablishing self-worth. This is not always easy. In fact, remorse, humiliation, self-hatred, self-condemnation, and other factors can make it seem impossible.

When we face this block, we have to ask, "Do we have the *right* to forgive ourselves?" Who are we to be so bold as to forgive ourselves? We may be acutely aware that there are those who believe that our offenses—great or small—should not be forgiven. And they surely don't believe we should be allowed room for self-forgiveness! They may hate the sight of us, and want us to keep out of their presence. They may insist we live forever after as lackeys, keeping our heads bowed, not speaking unless spoken to. They may want us to grovel some and crawl in shame. This, quite frankly, was my experience. And this type of pressure can make you feel as if you need to live the rest of your life like an abject slave, with no value at all.

Self-Love

Your offense may not be so "great" as to attract the spirit-crushing pressure I've described. But self-forgiveness can only begin when you realize that no matter how severe the offense, God will forgive if you seek forgiveness. After all, we are His creation, created perfectly but given free choice. Therefore, we must love ourselves even as He has loved us.

Esteeming ourselves worthy of God's forgiveness, though, can be a problem—and not just for the obviously hurting souls we might think of. I have always *liked* myself. I do not believe I have been either selfish or self-centered in this area. From my youth, I was taught that because God loves us, it is only natural that we love ourselves. I wish my experience was universally true, but it's not. Many people who have caused distress to others feel so remorseful that they not only dislike, but even hate themselves.

Reestablishing a love of self—as a person loved in God's sight—is essential for self-forgiveness.

Self-Honesty

After my arrest, I received hundreds of letters from friends and patients. All except one was supportive. That one negative letter was from a nurse. She was condemning and unforgiving. It made me acutely aware of the fact that there is always an element of society that is unforgiving. Even in the church you can encounter those who have an inability or unwillingness to forgive. Many of us wrongly believe that we must have 100-percent consensus about us, and can be overly sensitized by those who refuse to forgive. But the inability of others to forgive should never prevent or distract us from forgiving ourselves.

The pain and even the judgment placed on us by others can be turned to good effect, though. By that I mean it can cause us to contemplate—to look long and hard at—our failure or our sin, and admit we *have* done wrong. We must do this, whether we "meant" to harm others or not. Unless we honestly admit the harm we've caused by our words or deeds, we will see nothing for which to forgive ourselves.

Make no mistake: It takes bravery to confront ourselves with our misdeeds. Confronting ourselves cannot be avoided. Like self-love, self-honesty is essential.

Proper Confession

What we do next with the wrongdoing we discover in ourselves depends on the nature and impact of the offense.

Because sin and wrongdoing can have a ripple effect, it may have caused damage to many people. In my case, it was necessary to publicly apologize to my family, my church, my friends, my patients, and the medical community of which I'd been a part for thirty-five years. Because of the widespread publicity of my case, this apology was widely published. Even so, not everyone affected was aware of the public apology. The same nurse who wrote the letter to me later severely chastised me again for not publicly making a special apology to the medical community.

And those to whom you offer an apology may not accept it. There is no guarantee. All I can tell you is that rejection and misunderstanding is something you must bear.

On the other hand, it's not always necessary to "go public" with an admission of wrongdoing, even if the sin has some magnitude. The overly guilty person can assume a need to make a "big" confession, and in so doing commit overkill.

A perfect example is a man who had been unfaithful to his wife. The affair became known to the pastor and some church members. Based on the fact that "everyone" had the information, the governing body of the church felt that the man should confess his sin to everyone in the congregation. He agreed to this, and repented before a full church at a Sunday evening service.

On Wednesday evening, prior to the midweek service, he entered the sanctuary and committed suicide by gunshot. I did not know the man, but this much I do know about him: He must have believed that his sin was too great for God to forgive; he did not like himself for what he had done; the humiliation of the confession before the entire congregation was more than he could bear; he believed that his self-worth and self-esteem had been irreparably destroyed. He certainly did not forgive himself.

I also do not know the policy of that church, nor do I pass judgment on its leaders or congregation—but this much I do know: The man's sin was against his wife, and the exposure to the congregation was not necessary or scriptural. Jesus instructed us clearly: "If your brother sins against you, go and tell him his fault, between you and him alone" (Matthew 18:15, KJV). Some sins have an effect on one person or a few people, and nothing good is accomplished by a wholesale announcement.

Making a proper confession, then, is another essential of self-forgiveness.

Seek Forgiving Relationships

There is in all of us an urge to learn the worst about people and to pass on what we've learned. I believe this enables us to cover or suppress our own wrongdoing, or at least to convince ourselves that what we've done wrong is far less serious than the wrong we know others have done.

What this means, on a practical level, is that when we've sinned, others will want to hold us in unforgiveness, judgment, and condemnation. We'll encounter those who have no interest in seeing us heal, or being restored.

In her letter, the nurse I mentioned before quoted a doctor whose conviction was that I "should be punished for life." I contemplated that only for a moment. I wondered whether this doctor was hiding something. I practiced medicine long enough to know that mistakes made by doctors—even when unintentional, and even when they're not exposed by malpractice suits—do haunt them.

Russian novelist Aleksandr Solzhenitsyn said the world would be a great place "if there were only evil people committing cruel deeds and it were possible to separate them from the rest of us and to destroy them; but the line that separates good from evil cuts through the heart of every man, and who is willing to destroy a part of his own heart?"[5] But not everyone is willing to face the incredible potential for sin and wrongdoing that exists in each of us. Some level severe judgment as a way to boost their own self-esteem, seeing themselves as better when compared to others.

Even though others will judge us harshly and seek only to punish, we must seek to be healed and restored. I will repeat—we cannot let judgment and rejection get in the way of finding a new sense of self-esteem under God. We are God's sons and daughters, and we have roles to play in His work. We can help ourselves along, too, by seeking help with restoration from people who see life this way and who know the importance of esteeming others and helping them to esteem themselves.

Seek to Be Forgiving

Oddly enough, we can become more self-forgiving as we seek to understand and forgive the weaknesses of others, especially those who sin against us.

At the time of my arrest, a psychologist in our church was very unforgiving toward me, though I didn't know it at the time. Eleven years later, Grace and I were leading a seminar on forgiveness and this same psychologist was in attendance. After our first session, he came up and greeted me in a warm and complimentary manner. I was unaware of his reason for attending our seminar, given that he regularly participated in seminars of a similar nature. I was more surprised when he returned for the second day of the meetings.

A few weeks later, this man called and asked to come over for a visit. I had no idea as to his reason for coming. Not long into our visit, he confessed that he'd been unforgiving toward me when I was arrested, and continued to be so for all of those years. After hearing our story and so many examples of forgiveness, he felt compelled to come and ask for our forgiveness for his long delay in forgiving me. Could I understand his reticence to forgive? Of course. Could I forgive him? Certainly. We prayed, and we parted, both of us better off for his coming. I thought of two things as he walked down the sidewalk. First, what a great example he was—a well-known and distinguished individual humbling himself to both forgive and to ask for forgiveness. Second, that he was giving me an opportunity to practice offering the kind of forgiveness I needed.

To receive forgiveness is a relief; to offer it is to keep the blessing alive and growing within you.

Rest in Love

I want to offer you one final word about self-forgiveness, and to do so I must tell you something about my family and our home life.

We have lived in the same house for forty years. It is truly home for us—full of memories both happy and sad, great and small. From the time we moved into this house, whenever I crossed the threshold I'd say, "Daddy's home!" When the children were tiny they'd come toddling and we'd exchange warm hugs.

Soon they entered grade school, and when I came home I'd still say, "Daddy's home!" Even if they were reading or watching TV they'd look up and say, "Hi, Dad!" When they were in high school, I'd still say, "Daddy's home!"—and whoever wasn't at soccer or play practice would shout something in reply. Too quickly, the last child was in college, and I'd still enter, saying, "Daddy's home!" hoping at least Grace was in from work and might greet me.

When I was released from prison, my children thought it wise if only Grace went to receive me. The huge iron gates of the state's ancient prison opened to release this relieved but aching and needy soul.

I was free again . . . in one way at least.

As we drove back into our city, I was overwhelmed by the changes since I'd been gone. I felt unsettled. What else would I find changed—in my past friends? In my family?

As we pulled into our driveway, I felt a mixture of things . . . some comfort, and some unease. When I walked toward the front door I was stopped in my tracks by a wonderful sight.

My youngest daughter had made a poster and hung it on the front door to greet me. It said, simply, "Daddy's home!" And truly, I was.

What I want to tell you, from this experience, is that we can learn to forgive ourselves if we learn how to rest in love—God's love, and the love of those who are important in our lives. From these seeds of love, self-forgiveness will grow.

THE PRACTICE OF FORGIVING YOURSELF

As Herb's perspective shows us, sometimes our greatest challenge is to forgive ourselves.

Do you need to forgive yourself?

We can stop the self-abuse and rejection that masks hidden perfectionism and the wounded self-love that comes from pride. We can find esteem for ourselves again, and love ourselves as God loves us. We can stop excusing, and learn to profit from, our sins and mistakes by learning valuable lessons about ourselves and about life. With God's grace we can find gold in the ashes of our errors.

Recently, Grace met with a patient she's known since the woman was in her teens. She was then deeply depressed and bitter and later fell into habits that nearly cost her her life. She suffered shame and remorse over the several years of wasted time and life. Now she is on the path of spiritual maturity and health because she learned to move through regret, grief, and self-blame to experience self-forgiveness.

In looking back, this woman could see the road she'd had to travel. "Not a day goes by," she affirmed, "that I don't compare my old lifestyle to the new one. I thought I was free then to do anything I wanted. But now I'm really free to use the gifts I have, to do things that are truly great." Forgiving herself is allowing this woman to experience the wonder of peace and to sense that she's loved and valued more than she's ever known.

To forgive ourselves may be one of the most important steps we can take toward experiencing God's love. For this reason, self-forgiveness is not an optional side trip on the road to forgiveness, but rather lies at the heart of forgiveness.

CHAPTER NINE

FORGIVING GOD

M AYBE THIS CHAPTER TITLE JARS YOU A BIT. IT'S MEANT TO.
Many Christians might respond quickly, saying, "Forgive
God? What are you talking about? God doesn't sin or do evil, and
He isn't mean. God is holy, good, and perfect. So there's nothing
to forgive Him for."

For too many of us, though, that's a conditioned response that
comes straight from years of having sermon points and Bible verses
planted in the cortex of our brain. In our heads, we know truths
about God that are indeed true regardless of how we feel on a
given day. And yet at another, more subtle level—deep in our
spirit—we may not yet be so convinced. Truth be known, we
wrestle with the cognitive dissonance between what Christian doc-
trine tells us about God and what the painful circumstances of our
lives seem to tell us about Him—especially about His ability to
protect us and His willingness to care for us and keep us from
harm.

It's not our purpose to explore (much less try to resolve!) in
this chapter a deep theological question like, "Where is God when
bad things happen to good people?" But in our personal and

professional experience, everyone *experiences* hurt and even
anger toward God when trouble comes to them. If we express
those feelings out loud we're told, "You shouldn't feel that way.
God is good." Or we're treated to a theological answer by
Christian thought police—those who are uncomfortable in the
presence of someone who represents the great distance that can
exist between painful earthly realities and what the Bible says
about ultimate truths.

But the fact is, God is not uncomfortable with or dismayed
by our questions or feelings, not even our rawest emotions. We
do not need to protect Him. And in the end, to hide our feelings
from ourselves, thinking we're also hiding them from Him, cuts
us off from God's real ability to cleanse and heal the wounds we
sustain within.

For these reasons, we believe it's very important for you to
think long and hard about your feelings toward God as they relate
to the hard things that have occurred in your life. If we want to
heal and grow, it's crucial that we learn to be honest at a very deep
level, and not dodge the truth with rationalizations. Sure, we tell
ourselves that offenses are caused by other flawed human beings.
Or maybe no human agency is involved, and we try to chalk up
our injury to raw circumstance. We can come up with theological defenses and insist there's a difference between God's "active"
and His "permissive" will. But as the great missionary Amy
Carmichael put it, "The Lord had to allow it. Therefore, so far as
we are concerned He *did* it: He, Himself."[6]

Yes, the Bible makes it clear that God is holy, loving, and
good in all His ways. He is not the originator of evil. In fact, He
turns the evil and wrong that is aimed at us into blessing. As Amy
Carmichael would conclude in her next breath, "And all that He
does is good."[7]

Yet no matter how we cut it, even strong believers can have
serious questions about God's involvement in the hard circumstances of our life. After all, He *is* the creator and ruler of the

universe. Some of us dodge it. Others face it more readily. But there is something innate in every man and woman that immediately turns to God when bad things happen to us and asks, "Where were *You* when this was happening? Why did You allow it? Why didn't You intervene?"

AFRAID OF GOD

Many people find it very hard to admit they're angry, or even disappointed, with God. For one thing, it's not what "good Christians" do. For another—well, He's bigger and more powerful *and* the dispenser of blessings. What if our displeasure makes *Him* angry? Who wants to live looking over his shoulder all the time, waiting for God's judgment to strike?

This kind of fear is what the great missionary pastor Andrew Murray referred to as "craven" fear and not the true "fear of God" the Bible recommends to us. Many of us make the mistake of thinking the writers of Scripture are telling us to be "afraid of God" the way we're afraid of, say, getting cancer. Murray makes a great distinction for us when he says the true fear of God begins when we recognize that He is utterly trustworthy and powerful and good, and so *we fear to put our trust in anything besides God.*

A "craven" ungodly fear of God can be a block to questioning Him at all, especially if we're angry or unhappy. But admitting our questions, and even our emotions, to God is not "unChristian." Actually, if we take the step of facing God with our questions about His complicity in hurtful events that affect us, tremendous new things can happen in our lives. We'll find that "settling accounts" with God not only helps us to move beyond unforgiveness, it can offer us new wisdom and direction.

The first step, though, is to face the fact that even if we're not clear *how*, we count God as responsible in part, and involved in some way, in the events that harm us.

GETTING PERSONAL WITH GOD

About her years of marital distress, Grace says:

I prayed . . . a lot, and very *specifically*. I asked God to make a lot of changes in Herb. Soon I felt uncomfortable because I realized I was treating the Almighty as if He was an "order taker." I also began to get the message that if I wanted things to be different, *I* somehow had to change.

I didn't want to hear that, and that meant I was blocking truth. Whenever we do this, we cut ourselves off from a chance to grow and mature.

In any case, Herb didn't change, and I felt I was already doing my best. Slowly, without realizing it, I accumulated a lot of anger toward God. It was very hard to admit this even to myself. For a long time, I carried on those muttered conversations, as if I was talking about God when He wasn't around. Why didn't He answer me? Didn't He love me? Where was He, and what was He doing? What more could I do? God wasn't being fair.

When I most needed them, my friend Cecil Osborne's words to me hit both my heart and my head: "Perhaps we first become honest with God when we admit we are angry with Him!"

This was the first step in the change I believe God had been trying to tell me about. I hadn't been able to accept any truth about myself because I was so focused on trying to point out Herb's problems to God. But the message He was trying to send was that I was being dishonest with Him and with myself. How could I be in a strong, healthy relationship with others?

That one simple sentence, catching me when my guard was down, slipped the truth in. And once I was open and willing to consider it, a series of profound lessons came rapidly:

1. God requires absolute honesty—with myself and with Him.
2. God is big enough to be comfortable with my anger. He's not threatened by it.

3. Harboring anger alienates me in some measure from God, reducing my faith.
4. When I refuse to be completely honest with God, my relationship with Him stagnates. Eventually, it will grow cold, and maybe stop altogether.
5. God *wants* me to admit I need to forgive Him. He sees this problem in us when we refuse to see it in ourselves, and He works hard to call it to our attention. (I feel awed and humbled as I think about this.)

Many of us need to take this important first step in a new and deeper relationship with God. Hurt triggers anger; anger triggers unforgiveness. If allowed to go on long enough, unforgiveness turns to bitterness. If you ask someone who says he loves you, maybe countless times, to do something you desperately need, and he doesn't do it, sooner or later you have to conclude he doesn't love you and that you're unimportant to him. Nothing brings a flood of sadness, anger, and, later, even despair like discovering that words and promises of love were empty nothings.

Somewhere inside us, when we're harmed by another and God did not prevent it, we're tempted to believe that God's assurance that He loves us is just empty words.

Grace recognized that she was caught in a thought cycle that was spiraling downward spiritually: She'd ask. Her request seemed to be ignored. She'd stop asking. Then she'd feel God didn't love her. The relationship bonds were strained to breaking.

Speaking from past experience as the director of an intercessory prayer ministry, David also observes that many Christians get caught in this cycle: They pray hard, and when it doesn't "work" they give up. But in time the need becomes pressing again, or their frustration with God's non-reply lessens. Feeling a bit refreshed, they start the same prayers all over. When repeated rounds of praying for the same thing fail, some go on an almost endless search for the "right way" to pray. David wrote many letters in response to those who wrote to complain: "I'm so frustrated and angry at God. I keep asking Him for this one thing, and He just won't do it. Either He doesn't love me, or He just doesn't care. Tell me how to pray to get an answer. I'll do whatever you say."

Fairly often, Grace also counsels people who say, "God has left me. I pray and my prayers bounce off the ceiling. I feel abandoned by God."

Perhaps you need to "take stock" right at this moment, and seriously consider these questions:

Have you experienced loss, grief, or harm at the hands of another person? Do you hold God in some way responsible for allowing this offense to hurt you? Are you mad at God for not making life easier, or at least bearable?

At another level: Have you blamed God for "failing" to protect you or to answer your prayers? Can you see how this has made you lose faith even in a small measure? Have you stopped trusting Him, opting to "handle this myself in my own way, thank you"?

As we've observed, complete honesty with God is what's required if you are going to progress in your relationship with Him and in your own personal growth.

A NEW ROAD, A NEW DESTINATION

Those who get honest and admit their hard or hurt feelings toward God take a step down a surprising new road.

One man, a pastor, describes it this way: "I set out to admit to God I'd been angry at Him for allowing my son to get involved with the wrong crowd, which led to serious drug use and selling and then to a prison sentence. In fact, as I got going, I found myself railing against the _____ who got my son into drugs, and at God for allowing it and for not helping us discover the problem much, much earlier. And then an odd thing happened.

"I was in mid-sentence, telling God, 'I've spent my whole life serving You, and You couldn't even protect one of the most important people in my life.' As I said those words, something occurred to me.

"I'd had my life scripted out one way. And my version of my life didn't include having a son in prison. The thought occurred to me, *The problem is that you've been writing the script of your life all along. You've been telling yourself that you're willing to do God's will—and what if, in some mysterious way, this is part of God's will?*

"This set me back on my heels, I can tell you. It made me stop and think from a new perspective. The minute I allowed myself to take in this new possibility, a profound shift started taking place inside me. I saw how self-centered I'd been, imagining that my plan—no matter how 'godly' it looked—was still *my* plan for my life, and my son's life. In any case, the circumstances couldn't be changed. So what was I going to do now?

"I felt as though I was at a whole new beginning in my faith. Something like a second conversion. My *will* was being converted as I turned my life and my son's over to God again. I'd told God my life was under His care and direction, but now I saw that *I* was the one who'd made empty promises to God. What I'd really meant was, 'My life is under Your direction, as long as You do *this* and don't allow *that*.'

"In the depths of my soul I wasn't really allowing God to be God, or really living under His lordship. Now I had to choose to place myself and my son under His care and direction *for real*. Because I did that, I started on a new direction that's given me a deeper personal faith and taken me down new avenues of ministry as I bring God's love and concern to my son and to other guys in prison."

What this pastor is describing is the necessary return to *humility* that marks one of the greatest spiritual turning points in anyone's life. To discover humility means to take our true place in the order of things. It causes us to step out of God's position where we try to work out our own plan, and to agree to cooperate with the greater plan He is providentially working out. This kind of humility—surrender to and cooperation with God's plan—is extremely difficult for us because it grinds against our old way, which is to seek independence from God. And yet it's absolutely essential to the Christian life, and has been known for centuries as the "cardinal virtue" of Jesus Christ, who "humbled himself and became obedient to death—even death on a cross" (Philippians 2:8). Humility makes us true followers of Christ because it recreates in us His attitude of willing obedience to God.

Humility accepts that God saw the offense we would suffer . . . and that He made provision for it in His version of our life script. Humility sees that God took this action, all along knowing He would have to endure our hurt, anger, and possibly even our rejection of *Him,* as His will tried to cut through the hard knot of a secret, hidden will by which we try to govern our own lives. Humility rests in knowing that God must have known there was no other way to show us that our true god has been *our own will.*

Humility can also lead us, as it led the pastor whose story we've recounted, to begin following God, not only with a new spirit and attitude, but down a new path—possibly even to a new destination. For the first time, we may find that we are cooperating with God in "good works, which God prepared in advance for us to do" (Ephesians 2:10). We'll consider this important matter more in the final chapter.

For now, we need to understand a bit about who God is and how He works, and how we can forgive and reconcile with Him.

COMING TO TERMS WITH GOD

Letting go of offenses we've held against God requires us to do something we've alluded to already; that is, to take the humble position, to assume that God was right and good even as He allowed hard circumstances and losses to be written into the script of our personal history. Surely, we can think of times when we've been right, *known* we were right, and yet someone else thought we were dead wrong and maybe railed against us for our stance.

If you can't think of such a time, a simple example may help. Let's say you have a child who, though you have instructed against it, decides to smoke. He insists he "can't see anything wrong with it," and in fact it gets him acceptance and status with certain friends who are important to him. You still love him, and you try to steer him in the right direction—to quit smoking—in various ways. Now something else enters into play.

The minute you try to steer him the way you know is right for him to go, *tension* comes into the relationship. Even if he thinks there's the smallest inkling you might be right, there is an automatic resistance. To stop smoking would mean admitting he's wrong, and that would make him feel both *lesser* and like he's surrendering his will to your will—that he's *becoming subservient*.

Cancer wards are full of people who wish they knew why they didn't listen to loved ones who begged them to stop smoking, just as the world is full of people who wish they knew why they fight God so hard as He tries to guide and correct their life's course.

In the end, it comes down to our needing to choose between two positions: Either we know what's best for us, and we decide to choose our own plan, or we realize that a heavenly Father knows what's best for us, and choose to do whatever it takes to bend our will to His plan. *We must choose to trust, love, and follow Him, not only when it's obvious His plan will benefit us, but even when we cannot see any good in it.*

For many, this is where the battle gets intense. We feel we've been harmed by God's interference or negligence, and the retaliation impulse wants to see Him pay!

One way we retaliate is to continue holding on to angry, unforgiving feelings against God. We may believe we can "hurt" God the way it would hurt us if a loved one treated us to her bitter coldness.

Another way is to reject God, His ways, and His will—maybe even to hint that we're thinking about "wiping Him out of existence" by saying we're not sure there *is* a God.

Still another means of retaliation is to insist that because He didn't cooperate with our plan, we don't need to cooperate with *His* plan. We're free now to break as many of God's rules as we like—and He'd better not try to tell us we're in the wrong when *He's* the one who should answer for wronging *us*.

If you don't recognize these attitudes or stances, even in seed form, it may be that you have not been honest enough with yourself yet.

In the end, we have to face a great irony that lies at the bottom of it all. We have been wronged, and we've held God accountable in some measure for the offense. In part, the offense has raised to the surface an issue we could never see clearly *until* some painful incident jarred it loose and allowed it to float up into the light of day. That is the fact that we do not *naturally* respect God as God. Nor do we naturally want to know or cooperate with His will. We may have thought we did at some point, but it seems we're being asked to recognize the truth at a deeper level than before.

What we are saying, to boil this down to relational terms, is that there is a tendency in every one of us, no matter how long or how ardently we've been Christians, to choose to estrange ourselves from God more readily than we choose to trust Him or seek to understand Him. Please note: *We are the ones who operate this way—not God!*

Perhaps it's time to accept a more mature understanding of how God really works. We would like to share several bits of insight in this regard, believing that understanding releases us to accept and cooperate with Him, as well.

GOD IS LIKE NO ONE ELSE WE KNOW

There is no one else who is like God. Little wonder that we misunderstand Him and His ways.

Yet to know Him, truly, is to stand in awe. Consider: *God is the One—the only One—who knows all things.* Deep inside, many of us feel awed to think that God is so vast and eternal that He knows both the beginning and the end of all things. Even so, we hate to admit that with this kind of perspective God must also be the only one who knows what's best.

Be honest! There's something in each of us that *hates* to admit that. There's a piece of arrogance in us that wants to insist our way *must* be right. It's possible to have been a person of faith for decades and still encounter the old impulse that wants to get God to see things our way. Once we comprehend that God alone has the perspective from which to judge what's best for us, there can come a sense of relief. We are no longer responsible for trying to direct things.

God always wants what is best for us.

Grace says that going through the rigors of medical school and the early days in a practice, she wasn't convinced that a fair and loving Father wanted her to endure the sacrifices a medical career exacts. "Now," she says, "with the perspective of time, I look back over a life rich in experiences I couldn't have had in any other way. And I look forward to even more."

Carla had to forgive both an emergency room doctor and God when a misdiagnosis factored into her husband's death from bacterial meningitis. "In time, when I was able to get some distance from the pain and loss, I was amazed at how I'd grown as a human being—in personal strength, insight, compassion, and also in the wisdom that helps you accept what you cannot change.

"I do miss my husband, and I would never choose to go through this kind of pain," she concludes. "But I can also tell you I wouldn't trade anything for what this experience has done for me. I can see it was God's best choice for me."

God's way and His will for us are not always easy.

Grace also says that when she was a child her parents convinced her that it was "rewarding" to tackle really tough jobs and see them through to an excellent conclusion. That bit of motivational rhetoric was soon challenged. "As a senior in high school," Grace says, "Mr. Scott, my history teacher, often gave me an assignment that was different, and harder, than the class assignment. I worked very hard to earn his rarely given approval, but only at the end of the year did I overcome my shyness enough to ask, 'Why did you give me all those hard papers to write?' He replied, 'Because, Grace, I could see that you were up to harder work.' It was one of my highest compliments."

Our natural bent is to want life to be easy. When God gives us tough tasks and requires us to stretch and grow, it's because He knows the harder road will allow His strengths to come through in us. His presence with us, and His resources in us, make His assignments doable.

God is the author of tough love.
The God who allowed the Israelites to become slaves in Egypt also made them into a strong nation and delivered them. The God who allowed His Son Jesus to be nailed to a cross and die also raised Him from the dead and made Him Lord of all. Both are examples of God's version of tough love—a love that's greater and more durable even than the pain and hardships He allows, a love that is miraculous enough to make beauty out of ashes.

During Herb's early months in prison, he was extremely bitter. There was much in his case that had been handled unfairly. He was angry with Grace for divorcing him and with God for allowing it. He couldn't see anything good in what lay ahead for him behind bars. But one day a light dawned. He'd lived under immeasurable stress, making him a prime candidate for a heart attack. Despite the lack of humane treatment in prison, he had no responsibility. He had no big decisions, no big tasks, no accolades to earn. Maybe this was God's idea of tough love.

"I began to see that being in prison may have saved my life," Herb said. Since then, he's also seen it as God's way of giving him compassion for people who suffer in prison and purpose in serving them.

God's answer to prayer is not always "yes."
Many times God says, "No, that's not my plan." Or He may silently answer, "Not now!"

David, a wise eight-year-old Grace knows, prayed very hard for a sick relative to live. Instead, he died. Some months later, the little boy's Sunday school teacher asked the class, "Has God ever answered 'yes' to your prayers?" Each child had a great example of the answers they'd enjoyed.

Then came the hard question. "Has God ever said 'no' to your prayers?" David was the only child who raised his hand. "I asked God to let my uncle live. But God said, 'no.' Uncle Alan died."

Many of us know the feeling of powerlessness that comes when God doesn't live up to our wishes and demands. But if God is to be God in our lives, we must grow beyond an immature expectation that He will always spare us from hearing the answer "no."

God Awaits Our Return

Chad is a great guy who has struggled throughout his life with fears and failures. Though he is gifted in many ways, his life did not begin to reflect the talents buried within. He suffered broken relationships, lost jobs, and experienced a devastating lack of self-confidence. It took years for him to understand himself and realize what was holding him back.

When Chad was only four, he always wanted to be with his daddy, a big and powerful man. Chad would tinker near his dad in the wood shop of their basement. Chad would pick up the wood scraps left when his dad sawed, and nail the pieces together. Then he proudly held them up for his dad's inspection.

Instead of praising his son's creativity, his dad yelled at him for wasting the nails. Sometimes, just for "bothering" him,

Chad's father flew off the handle and treated him to a violent spanking. Coldly, he'd tell his son, "Go away and leave me alone so I can get my work done."

Alone, hiding behind some shelves in a corner of the basement, Chad sat in acute and abject pain. The one man in all the world that he most wanted to be with, and to be like, despised and rejected him.

It wasn't too great a stretch for him to believe that as a human being, he was "rejectable"—maybe even rejected by God.

Years later, as a man, Chad cried bitter tears as these painful memories and feelings returned. Not only that, he could see how his sense of rejection and worthlessness had crippled his creativity and held him back all his life. "Where was God then? How could a loving heavenly Father allow any man to treat his little boy like that?" God seemed as hard and cruel as his father had been.

Grace, who was counseling Chad, recognized that he was reliving the root cause of his life's struggles—his inability to thrive emotionally and spiritually, and to use the gifts and talents he possessed. She also knew of a certain source of healing for him. First, she led him to a Scripture in which Jesus said, "I am with you always" (Matthew 28:20).

"Chad," she said, "Jesus didn't reject or abandon you. He was with you in that lonely corner of the basement. If you'd been able to see and hear Him—what do you suppose He would have said and done?"

Chad's look of anguish softened. "I never thought about Him being *with* me. I believe He would have put His arm around my shoulder and told me not to feel so bad. I think He would have . . . , " and here his voice choked. "I think He would have picked up those little nailed-together pieces of wood and told me I did a great job."

God, he saw, was *not* like his dad after all. He was able to "forgive" God—more rightly put, to recognize that God was actually trying to work in a much bigger situation that extended beyond his own need for healing. And so Chad saw that God was not to blame, not the one who needed forgiveness.

They went on to discuss the situation from a whole-family perspective, and Chad was able to begin looking at it from the standpoint of a healing adult, not a hurting child. He knew his dad had suffered many hurts while growing up. Those hurts had calloused his heart, and so the unhealed pain inflicted by his own father was the same pain he passed on to Chad. Seeing this, he was able to forgive his father, too.

Whether Chad's healing benefits his dad or prevents pain from being passed on to his own children, letting go of the hurt he believed God had allowed ended the continuous wounding that came from the pain of the past. And now, a little at a time, Chad could move on to health and spiritual maturity.

CHAPTER TEN

RESTORATION

UNTIL THIS POINT, WE'VE EMPHASIZED THE PROCESS OF FORGIVEness that leads to the letting go of offenses. This effort is necessary if we are to gain some objective distance from both the offense and the offender. It's this objectivity that helps us to come out from under the relentless grinding of loss, grief, hurt, anger, bitterness, and distrust that injury brings. Only when we can let go of the impulse to revenge that keeps us trapped in the past, only when we can understand and release, does our inner being and our thinking stand apart from, or "rise above," the event. It's then that our ability to live supernaturally above the event empowers us and sets us free.

If a major offense has knocked us down and left us reeling under its effects, the process of forgiveness helps us get up again and regain our balance.

Yet there is another part of forgiveness, a step that seems utterly impossible when we've been knocked flat on the ground: It's the step in which we *seek the good of the offender.*

STANDING IN A NEW POSITION

Letting go of a serious offense does not release us from further involvement with the offender, especially if the offender is someone with whom we had a close relationship before the offense. Issues do not go away, and people do not necessarily change just because they've been forgiven. Sometimes they do, and sometimes they don't. Even if there is no reason to see the offender again, it may be that something inside tells us that our dealings are not done.

We begin to sense that we are "called"—being given an opportunity. Forgiveness works into us a greater heart than the one that used to beat in our chests—the heart of the one who, while we were yet sinners, while we were still His enemies and hated Him, nonetheless loved, sought, and gave Himself for us (see Romans 5:6-8). We believe He asks us to go out with Him on His shepherd missions, seeking those still lost to His love, mercy, and grace.

This cooperative mission with God is not to be entered into lightly, or before we're ready. Seeking to restore the serious offender to a way of living that brings health and maturity requires strength and wisdom. A nervous, neurotic, *too*-quick attitude—"I forgive you, let's not deal with this uncomfortable unpleasantness again"—is not cooperation with the work God likely wants to do to restore the offender. To seek her good is best done, and perhaps can only be done, from a position of stability. We must feel balanced again, and hold a solid vision of ourselves as whole (or at least healing) and in cooperation with God.

Frankly, this is where many of us get into trouble. Sometimes our "Christian" sense of what we "should" do as believing people causes us to try to seek the good of an offender prematurely, while we're still reeling and in pain from the gash the offense has dealt us. Maybe others have pushed us, saying, "You *have* to forgive."

Karl, both a young and a new Christian, forgave his pastor for speaking openly about Karl's struggles with sexuality for which he'd sought counsel. He'd been told forgiving was "the Christian thing to do." But far-reaching damage had been done, both to Karl personally and to the pastor's reputation. Distrust of the man spread rapidly, resulting in a bitter church split. No one led Karl and the pastor through a process of forgiveness, through steps of accountability, with an eye on *restoration*. Had this been done, the single offense might not have continued to gain in power, bringing far greater destruction.

Jeri held $32,000 in overdue bills for consulting work, and the firm that was months in arrears asked her to "forgive" them for being "behind." Because she was a Christian she felt she had to say, "Sure, I forgive you," and not press for the money, both because the firm was struggling to make it and because she "wanted to be a good witness." She'd thought about demanding a meeting with them in the presence of one other Christian businessman who could moderate, but her pastor talked her out of it. ("You need to forgive and go on.") Shortly, she discovered they'd never planned to pay the bill and had scammed others, too. A firmer stance might have kept others from injury.

It is certainly honorable and right to set our will to "do the right thing," and even push ourselves to use forgiving words and actions as soon as possible. This helps us take hold of the *intention* to forgive, even as we begin the process we've outlined. Intention is the beginning, and it also seems to be all we need to draw God's assistance.

But as we've seen, intention needs to be followed by steps that make it real in terms of both inner and outer reality. Otherwise, our best Christian intention is only a chimera and our forgiveness can be as thin and insubstantial as a wisp of smoke. Inside, we *say*, "I forgive," wishing we *could* forgive, all the while crossing and recrossing the boundary line within us that needs to be firm in order for a solid decision to be made. Another offense comes and, like a bitter wind, drives away our weak resolve.

A quick, weak, insubstantial offer of forgiveness never offers the offender the important chance he needs — that is, the chance

to recognize the damaging effects of the offense, to accept responsibility, to effect changes in his life, and to make restitution. This
is the repentance Jesus calls offenders to, and calls us to work along
with Him. Who can speak more authoritatively than we can —
with insight and experience — to the one who has offended?

This is why a *solid decision* both to forgive and restore is the
key. Until this set position is reached, we're wise to say, "I want
to forgive, but I need time and a chance to work this through."
Much of the "working through" is what you've read to this point;
it's the process that brings us to balance and spiritual solidness.

A New Horizon

Once we've reached a firm resolve, we can find that another
transformation takes place. Before, these words from Jesus, the
Master of forgiveness, did not make sense:

> "Do not resist an evil person. If someone strikes you on the
> right cheek, turn to him the other also." (Matthew 5:39)

He goes on to name other injuries that can befall us, taking
our dignity, peace, material possessions, and freedom, and then
tells us to respond to "taking" in an opposite spirit, saying,
"*Give . . .* " (5:42, emphasis added). Before, when we were in the
first throes of the injury, this seemed both ridiculous and impossible. Now, we find ourselves looking at a new horizon.

Before, we wanted to resolve the matter of our own need for
healing from the injury. Now we see a new possible goal. We no
longer see the offender as someone who only deserves punishment, but as someone in need of repentance — not only in the
spiritual sense, but in the sense of recognizing a great need for
help, healing, and growth in maturity. We feel ourselves *wanting*
to make a step of generosity toward the offender. We want to see

good come to the individual, and not "evil for evil."

To our own surprise and wonder, *taking Jesus' route of forgiveness has changed us from within.*

Now we find an impulse in us that's willing to risk, to try what is, naturally speaking, unthinkable and ridiculous. We're willing to stand up to the voices that say, "This is a lost cause," and "You're wasting your time," and even, "There must be something wrong with you." The generous, strengthening presence of God with us makes us seek the health and restoration of the offender. To the unbelieving, the merely judgmental, and the double-minded doubtful mind, this makes no sense. As Paul observed, to many, Jesus' gospel of forgiveness and restoration is "foolishness" (1 Corinthians 1:18-20,27).

To us, it has become the next step we know we *must* take if we're going to continue experiencing this new, strong, healthier way of life that's buoying us from within.

Impossible as it seemed at first, we know now that we must turn our attention from ourselves and see, if possible, that good comes to the one who wronged us. Paul taught, in the same generously forgiving spirit as Jesus, "If it is possible, as far as it depends on you, live at peace with everyone" (Romans 12:18). Paul was both wise and kind to give us those qualifiers! As we know, it's not within our power to guarantee change in another's heart. Some people are incorrigible and will never change. The thing is, *we don't know who the incorrigibles are!* That's not our judgment call to make.

For various reasons—marriage, family or friendship ties, even choice—we'll find ourselves in ongoing relationships with those who have harmed us. Far from being weak or codependent, we can act from strength to offer our offenders the same way of peace and spiritual health we're discovering. We can offer to help them experience restoration.

Where do we begin?

SETTING AND MAINTAINING FIRM BOUNDARIES

We can only offer help, as we've said, from a position of emotional and spiritual strength.

We get that strength as we rely on God's help in establishing the healthy boundaries that make for spiritual wholeness and good relationships. When we fail to abide by these boundaries, we harm other people. When we allow someone to trample our boundaries, we remain victims. This is why we must first establish healthy boundaries within ourselves. Then, "if it is possible," we may be able to help others in this task, as well.

The Need to Maintain Personal Boundaries

A bit of hindsight can help us here: Looking back, we can see that the process of forgiveness has shown us how to establish firm boundaries within ourselves. Our task as we seek restoration is to maintain those boundaries. To set a boundary is to come into agreement with our own perceptions—wrong was done—and it establishes a barrier to prevent further damage. It is to say, "You've crossed a line and injured me. It stops here."

Now we can see why it's in the best interest of the offenders to recognize and respect boundaries, too. Whether they have a serious defect in this area, or selfishly allowed themselves a momentary lapse, the result was the same: They trampled on us. For their sake, they need a sense of *boundary respect* restored.

Boundary respect is restored when we give offenders the clear message: "What you did wronged me, because it . . ." and here we must state the specific harm done, such as, "destroyed trust," "physically hurt me," "made me lose money," or "cost me my job."

The Need to Help the Offender Recognize and Respect Boundaries

Showing the offender how a lack of boundary respect caused injury offers him the chance to recognize full responsibility for what he has done.

"Telling some guy he 'hurt' me feels weak and kind of . . . *womanly,*" Frank argues. He was cheated in a business deal by some Christian "brothers." "They know what they did wrong. I told them they were crooks and they should be ashamed to call themselves Christians. I prefer to let it go now. Isn't that the smart thing to do?"

In a word, no. Frank, himself a Christian, was blind to the fact that all he'd done was to return abuse, and then abandon an opportunity to lay out terms by which relationship balance could be restored.

Consider it this way. What we've encountered is the offender's self-centered "smallness." The offense has given us a chance, so to speak, to know the offender's weaknesses and shortcomings, maybe better than the individual knows. Who better than we to share how to have a healthy, equitable, maturing human relationship in this regard?

Lynn came to a point in forgiving her father for abusiveness where she realized she, better than any pastor or therapist, had the insight to tell him exactly what was wrong inside him. Using a counselor's assistance for support, she was able to lay out the specific terms required in order for him to have a healthy relationship with her now. In the counseling session, he hung his head in remorse: "I never imagined that my own daughter was going to have to be a parent to me. You're teaching me more about strength and love than anything I ever taught you."

Growth Through Seeking Restoration

When we help to set boundaries and terms, it can yield great benefits. Being a "victim" makes one feel weak; lashing out with retaliatory or condemning words accomplishes nothing, even magnifies one's sense of powerlessness. Setting the boundaries and terms of healing as a step in forgiving reestablishes our sense of strength. As well, it gives the offender concrete steps to take if that person, too, wants spiritual and emotional health in a restored relationship. Until we see this interaction to be as important as it is, we may not realize how bad it is for any offender to get by with hurting others.

Learning how to work with another in this business of restoration is a growth step of profound importance for every one of us. And we want to add this: *Facing an offender with terms that will reestablish the relationship on healthy terms is especially important for victims of chronic abuse.* Consider this:

Abuse victims unknowingly stay in the role of victim in most of their relationships. They do so not by choice, but because abuse has taught them certain unhealthy relationship habits. The abuse of most long-term victims began in childhood. Then, they were helpless and cowered in fear. They learned to avoid confrontations—or if they confronted and were met with anger or more abuse, they crumbled inside and accepted this further mistreatment. They had no patterns for healthy arguments, thought-provoking disagreements, and the fair negotiation techniques we described earlier. They crossed lines inside themselves over and over, sometimes passively accepting abuse, at other times mustering a little strength—but not enough to put it to an end. These unfortunate strugglers often live as adults in silent resentment, sometimes carrying a "martyr" attitude that makes them believe they're strong and heroic for "putting up with it." In fact, they are estranging themselves from reality, from themselves, and even in a sense from God, who is urging them on to maturity but whose promptings they ignore.

If you have suffered chronic abuse, you will most likely need help in establishing terms in order to know what's right and what's wrong in any given relationship. If you are a parent, you will need this help not only for yourself but so that you can teach and reinforce this understanding in your children. We urge you to get that help from a wise and trained professional.

The bottom line, however, is that taking this step will help you regain strength where you have lacked steadiness, or maybe even been weak and helpless.

ON HOLD UNTIL FURTHER NOTICE

There is a tool that's useful in renegotiating relationships, and it can be especially helpful in communicating with those we're offering to guide back onto a healthy spiritual path.

If the offender is resistant, or even more aggressive, we can remain focused and strong by giving that person a clear signal: This relationship, or dialogue, is on hold until he or she is willing to respect your need for new ground rules.

Jeri, who was cheated by Christian businessmen, ultimately realized she needed to take responsible steps in relation to her offenders. She wrote them a letter reminding them that people in their community often asked her to recommend, or vouch for, these particular men. She said, "I'm willing to work with you to resolve this offense. But until then, I will be telling your potential customers, 'I don't recommend you work with them at this time.'" Telling them the relationship was on hold—along with her important business recommendation—woke these men up to what they were doing. They phoned and asked how they could reconcile.

Here are two more examples to show how the on-hold technique can work in everyday settings:

Vivian's husband for years subjected her to verbal abuse every time she tried to discuss their budget. She was considering divorce when a counselor challenged her to consider forgiveness and restoration instead. The next time he began his attack, Vivian stood up. "I'm going for a walk. I won't talk to you when you're like this. I want calmness and respect. When you're ready to do that we can talk about the budget issues we need to settle."

Brad tried to raise important issues with his wife, but could never make headway. The minute Brenda felt threatened she turned the situation around and unloaded all the pent-up irritations she'd harbored for months. They separated, and it was in counseling that they learned about taking "timeouts."

The next time Brad tried to talk and got resistance, he said,

"Brenda, I really want to hear your beefs about me. But I'd like us to talk out my issues *just once*. I have to know you're really hearing me, and that you care about what's bothering me. Then I swear I'll listen to the things that bug you about me. But if you won't respect my need—can't you see we have no place to go?" Then he took a drive, and when he returned he found Brenda ready and willing to go along with his terms.

Using this relational tool can make all the difference in the process of forgiving offenses and in restoration.

Think of it this way. Putting a hold on a relationship or dialogue is like closing a door (stopping the attack) but not locking it (judging and dismissing the attacker). Calling a halt allows you some time and distance when you need it, in order to remain clear-thinking, calm, and therefore strong. It allows the other party to experience you as a healthy boundary setter, and gives a consequence to think about. In fact, the offender may need to experience being cut off and taken in hand as a consequence of lack in boundary respect. She may be used to dominating, controlling, and getting her way in life in general, or maybe only in the relationship with you. Now she is learning that relationships cannot be run on one person's terms only.

What we've just described is the way in which those all-important relationship bonds—trust and respect—begin to repair. Now the offender can begin, if willing, to make a way back to the offended across the chasm of harm done. We have helped them define the important next step.

REPARATION

Offering forgiveness *and* renegotiating the relationship will lead us to discussing *reparation*. We believe giving the offender a chance to make reparation does two important things. First, it allows him to demonstrate that he wants to repair the relationship; second, it allows him to begin practicing the relationship terms that create those healthy bonds of trust and respect.

We say *reparation* because it is always possible to work at repairing a relationship, while it is not always possible to "pay restitution." An offender can repay damages to us, like stolen funds—but in fact there is really no way to "repay" things like lost years of our lives, debilitating injuries, or the death of a loved one.

Clara's encounter with the young man jailed for life for killing her only son presents a good example of what reparation can look like and what it can accomplish.

Clara's Christian faith moved her to seek help in forgiving the young man, Terry, who shot her son to death in a convenience store robbery. Desperate for money to support his cocaine habit, Terry had pulled the trigger six times and left her son to die, making off with $39. The cold-blooded nature of the crime erased the possibility of parole.

Eventually, in the months she worked through forgiving Terry, she asked a prison chaplain to arrange a meeting. To the amazement of her friends and family, she continued to seek a relationship with Terry, who, though cold and wary at first, began to respond.

Then came the day Terry crumbled. Doubled-over in spasms of emotional pain, Terry begged Clara's forgiveness. Clara, too, was weeping as she said, "You already know I forgive you, son." Together they prayed as Terry begged God's forgiveness and accepted Christ's sacrifice for his sins. Clara saw her son's killer enter the kingdom of God that day.

But the work wasn't through.

On her next visit, Terry asked Clara, "What can I ever do to make up for what I've done?"

Some might have answered, "Nothing. Jesus paid it all"— confusing Christ's atoning work on the cross with the very real human need to grow in spiritual responsibility and purpose. Zaccheus was clearly forgiven by Christ for robbing the taxpayers, but Jesus allowed him to repay his victims four times what he'd taken (see Luke 19:1-10).

Clara had already thought about the importance of reparation. There was a counseling program she asked Terry to enter for his own sake. And there was another program that brought troubled kids into prison to meet with inmates. "I want you to volunteer to meet with those kids and tell them your story," said Clara. "Help them see the kind of consequences they'll face if they don't change their behavior."

To this day, Clara and Terry stay in touch, praying together for the young men and women Terry speaks to from prison. Terry's efforts at reparation have changed his life, brought help to dozens of teenagers, and helped Clara with her healing as well.

This is a dramatic story, for sure. The reparations we negotiate may be simpler, but just as crucial.

It restores self-respect and cements the commitment to change and growth.

Doing the "Impossible"

"Iron sharpens iron," says the proverb (27:17). When we establish personal boundaries, boundary respect in others, and terms of reparation, we act in spiritual strength to restore spiritual strength in another. What was weak, sick, immature, and abusive in them is not only called into account but called to health.

As we've noted before, there are circumstances that will prevent us from seeking restoration with the offender. Death, unwillingness, inability to locate someone from the past—these may keep us from actively seeking the good of the one who injured us. Then we rely on the process of forgiveness to bring good to our own lives.

Still, there are times when the relationship has suffered so much damage we're tempted to say, "I can forgive. But restoring the other person is probably impossible. And a 'new relationship'? *Out of the question!*"

Certainly, these are thoughts and feelings Grace experienced, until she recognized the open door that stood before her: The chance to be spiritual "iron" in the life of her fallen, broken ex-husband.

"I had to come to terms with my own lack of faith," says Grace. "I knew that if I couldn't believe that 'with God all things are possible,' then I would have to quit my counseling career and give up my faith.

"On the other hand, if all things *are* possible with God, I had to believe that even our destroyed marriage could be restored on new terms."

Today, Grace and Herb stand amazed at the restoration that has taken place in their relationship.

Here are the steps that led to their restoration:

The shock of Herb's arrest effectively turned him around. The clang of prison bars was his wake-up call and made him come to terms with the consequences of his choices. Forgive the pun, but in this case iron truly sharpened iron.

Grace recognized that she could still choose her role, even in this crushing event. She could choose the "moral high ground," and act superior; or the role of "wounded victim," and act out her grudge; or even play "the nice Christian," and "forgive"—without recognizing the God-given opportunity to seek Herb's healing, repentance, and restoration.

Grace was honest in counting the cost of hurts done to her. Because of that she experienced her pain "up front"—which kept her from being ambushed by unresolved feelings later, when they might have exploded out of her as ammunition in meetings with Herb.

Herb recognized that Grace had not come to gloat, or merely to list his sins and wrongs. He recognized in her a supernatural response—the offer to help restore him. This incredible offer could be nothing else but the mercy and grace of God, coming to him through a human vessel.

Grace was able to help Herb set new boundaries regarding

acceptable and unacceptable behavior. He recognized that these terms were for his own good, as well as hers.

Together they renegotiated the terms of their relationship. Eventually, Grace's part in their relationship weaknesses could be addressed, along with Herb's.

Today, they continue to relate by practicing active *problem solving,* instead of no-win *power struggling.*

Together, they've agreed to dialogue until it's clear how one has hurt the other, and how reparations can be made.

Today, both say, "We didn't know this kind of spiritually maturing relationship was really possible."

Perhaps you can see from these steps that working toward restoration brought a healthy new balance to this relationship—a balance called *mutuality.* Achieving mutuality means that a relationship has been restored so that a healthy give and take is going on.

RECONCILIATION

One of the most significant moments in a spiritually maturing life occurs when we can stop thinking of ourselves as the "offended" and thinking of others who injure us as "offenders." It signals that we've come to a new place and accepted a new identity for ourselves. It signals that we've made achievements under the mentoring of the Master of forgiveness, and that we recognize our place at His side as the gospel of mercy and grace for sinners is brought to this fallen world and those imprisoned by sin and self-centeredness. Now we can begin to see ourselves as God sees us—laborers together with Him (see 1 Corinthians 3:9)—in seeking and restoring His lost ones.

This is something the world can never understand.

But we can understand. And we can live with the same vision of ourselves that the apostle Paul had when he wrote that God "reconciled us to himself through Christ, and gave us the ministry of reconciliation" (2 Corinthians 5:18).

Throughout Christian history, believers have understood that there are two roads one may follow through life. Which of the two roads we choose determines the way we live, and whether we'll experience the peace, freedom, rest, and wisdom of God within ourselves. It is this inner knowing that Jesus spoke of when He said, "The kingdom of God is within you" (Luke 17:21).

A love that seeks the good of the other, even an offender, is the law of that kingdom. That is to say, when the love and forgiveness of God govern our hearts, they will also govern our outer actions and our words. Love will, literally, rule our lives.

There is no question that it's hard work to bring the loving rule of God into hearts that are willful to begin with and made even harder when being wronged tempts us to believe we have "good reason" to be unforgiving. In fact, as Christians throughout the centuries have always known, it requires a life of learning how to cooperate with God in order to make His loving responses ours.

We hope that this book has helped you to begin, or to take further steps, toward spiritual maturity in Jesus Christ—a maturity that helps you to be a person in whom Jesus' own forgiving spirit lives.

It's our hope and prayer that each time you forgive you will not only experience peace, but that you will have a stronger sense of God's great heart and the grace with which He includes us in the plan to restore all men and women to Himself.

NOTES

1 Interview on *Good Morning America*, American Broadcasting Company; October 4, 1999.

2 *Webster's New World Dictionary Student Version*, Second College Edition, "talon."

3 *Merriam-Webster Dictionary Student Version*, (New York: Pocket Books, 1974), "forgive".

4 Well-meaning spiritual people sometimes teach, wrongly so, that forgiving means allowing the offender to escape the experience of justice. Those who have been seriously, even criminally, harmed are often told, "Just forgive." This leaves them in a weak and confused position in which they can be victimized again and again, if not by the same offender then by others. It also leaves them to be victimized spiritually and psychologically by the pressure from their own sense of justice that tells them, correctly, that they are right to be offended—and by the countering pressure of others who insist they are wrong, or not "spiritual," to want the serious criminal offender brought to justice.

It is our position that offering personal forgiveness *and* insisting that the offender also experience justice are *compatible* and *balancing* urges. The experience of justice is just as important as the experience of forgiveness, in the spiritual reformation of the serious criminal offender. Just as important, and in keeping with the purpose of this book, replacing the desire to punish with the desire to reform (if possible) is the path that leads to healing and wholeness for the offended or victimized person.

5 Aleksandr I. Solzhenitsyn, *Gulag Archipelago* (San Francisco: Harper-Collins, 1991).

6 David Hazard, ed., *You Are My Hiding Place: A 40-Day Journey in the Company of Amy Carmichael* (Minneapolis: Bethany House Publishers, 1991), p. 56.

7 Hazard, p. 56.

About the Authors

Dr. Grace Ketterman graduated from the University of Kansas Medical School in 1952, and practiced in pediatrics for many years. She subsequently completed a residency in child psychiatry. She has been in the business of helping troubled families for over forty years. For many years, she was the Director and then the Medical Director of the Crittenton Center in Kansas City, Missouri.

Dr. Ketterman is the mother of three and the grandmother of four. She is now in private practice, consults with Crittenton and with school districts in the Kansas City area, and is a popular speaker both locally and nationwide. She is the author of fourteen books, including *Mothering in All Ages and Stages, Depression Hits Every Family,* and *Parenting the Difficult Child.* Her concern for, and interest in, families is based in her deep spiritual faith, which she describes as "practical and loving."

David Hazard is a bestselling and award-winning author and the founder of *The New Nature Institute,* an organization that promotes the study of Christian spiritual practices as they relate to physical health and wellness.

Formerly, David was acting director for Breakthrough, an international intercessory prayer ministry, and senior editor of the NavPress Spiritual Formation Line.

He is known to readers for such titles as *No Compromise: The Keith Green Story* and *Blood Brothers,* and he is the creator of the acclaimed classics devotional series, Rekindling the Inner Fire, and the Lifeskills for Men series. Currently, he is developing a series of health and wellness books.

David lives in Virginia with his wife, MaryLynne, and three children — Aaron, Joel, and Sarah Beth.

MORE HELP FROM NAVPRESS.

Bold Love

The kind of love modeled by Jesus Christ has nothing
to do with unconditional acceptance or manners. Far from
helping you "get along" with others, *Bold Love* introduces the
outlandish possibility of making a significant, life-changing
impact on family, friends, coworkers—even your enemies.
(Dr. Dan B. Allender and Dr. Tremper Longman III) $14

The Cry of the Soul

For the person who struggles with negative emotions
such as anger, fear, or jealousy, *The Cry of the Soul* tells us
how even negative emotions can lead us closer to God.
(Dr. Dan B. Allender and Dr. Tremper Longman III) $18

Get your copies today at your local bookstore,
through our website at www.navpress.com, or by
calling (800) 366-7788. Ask for offer **#6067.**